מסורה

ArtScroll Series®

Rabbi Nosson Scherman / Rabbi Meir Zlotowitz

General Editors

A Happier

Published by

Mesorah Publications, ltd

You

A Teenager's Guide to Happiness and Confidence

Roiza D. Weinreich

FIRST EDITION
First Impression . . . November 1995

Published and Distributed by
MESORAH PUBLICATIONS, Ltd.
4401 Second Avenue
Brooklyn, New York 11232

Distributed in Europe by
J. LEHMANN HEBREW BOOKSELLERS
20 Cambridge Terrace
Gateshead, Tyne and Wear
England NE8 1RP

Distributed in Israel by
SIFRIATI / A. GITLER — BOOKS
4 Bilu Street
P.O.B. 14075
Tel Aviv 61140

Distributed in Australia & New Zealand by
GOLDS BOOK & GIFT CO.
36 William Street
Balaclava 3183, Vic., Australia

Distributed in South Africa by
KOLLEL BOOKSHOP
22 Muller Street
Yeoville 2198, Johannesburg, South Africa

THE ARTSCROLL SERIES ®
A HAPPIER YOU
© Copyright 1995, by MESORAH PUBLICATIONS, Ltd. and Mrs. Roiza D. Weinreich
4401 Second Avenue / Brooklyn, N.Y. 11232 / (718) 921-9000

ISBN:
0-89906-589-9 (hard cover)
0-89906-590-2 (paperback)

Printed in the United States of America by Noble Book Press Corp.
Bound by Sefercraft Quality Bookbinders, Ltd., Brooklyn, N.Y.

Acknowledgments

I'd like to thank the many people who provided ideas and support during the process of writing this book.

It's difficult at times to see the qualities of those closest to us, those whom we see every day. I have worked with over 200 young adults on this book. I admire their honest struggle to learn and grow. They sincerely want to do the right thing. Their good-natured generosity is amazing.

My appreciation goes to my sister Manya Fisher. This book would not have been possible without her help. Thank you, Miss Frenkel, Rebbetzin Gitel Herbst, Fayge Silverman, all the workshop participants and all the girls from Bais Yaakov High School, Yeshiva of Brooklyn, Shulamis and Prospect Park — Bnos Leah, who contributed carefully thought-out ideas and suggestions. I'm sorry I can't list everyone's name here but your contribution added a beautiful dimension to the book. Those contributions which are unsigned were submitted by individuals who wish to remain anonymous. There are a few names missing in the book. Please forgive me if your name was omitted by mistake. If you would like your name included and you notify me, it will appear in the next edition.

Mrs. Ethel Gottlieb was thorough yet gentle while editing. Her insight and creative ideas added profoundly to the book. It was truly delightful and encouraging to work with her.

Gratitude goes to Rabbis Meir Zlotowitz and Nosson Scherman for putting their faith in this project and for their help in bringing about the impressive success of my first two books. My special thanks to Rabbi Sheah Brander whose expert knowledge made the book complete. My sincere appreciation to Rabbi Avrohom Biderman, Mrs. Faygie

Weinbaum, Mrs. Mindy Stern, Mrs. Bassie Gutman, Mrs. Devori Bick and Udi Herskovits of the ArtScroll staff. I consider it a privilege to participate in the ArtScroll Series.

My parents, Mr. and Mrs. Moshe Perlman, and my mother-in-law, Mrs. Pearl Weinreich, have encouraged and sustained all my various undertakings. I hope they will always have *nachas* from all their children and grandchildren. The first one to read significant portions of the book was my husband, Faivel. From the beginning he's helped me decide many times what will work and what won't and has patiently encouraged me not to give up when I faced minor setbacks.

The most successful person I ever met was my grandmother, Chava bas Shaul A"H, who was active and self-sufficient until she passed away at the age of 89. She was an aristocrat of the last generation. Her aristocracy was not measured by possessions, fame, or college degrees but rather by her nobility of spirit. Every day, the love in her heart created happiness in a tangible way. Her real-life example was the foundation for the ideas in this book.

I thank Hashem for the wide acceptance of my first books and for the *zechus* to reach thousands of people around the world with Torah ideas that helped them to become better Jews.

ויהי נעם ה׳ אלקינו עלינו ומעשה ידינו כוננה עלינו ומעשה ידינו כוננהו, *May Hashem's Presence and Satisfaction rest upon us. May Hashem complete our efforts and assure their success. May the work of our hands establish Hashem's Kingdom on earth* (*Tehillim* 90:17).

Table of Contents

Introduction: What Does Self-Esteem Mean for You?

❧ I Have Self-Esteem When . . .

Check any box that provides a good definition for you.

☐ I know that the world was created for me.
☐ I am aware of my talents.
☐ I know I have choices.
☐ I understand that every day I am a new person.
☐ I feel happy to be myself.
☐ I am willing to risk and learn.
☐ I pay attention to my feelings.
☐ I take on new responsibilities.
☐ I thank Hashem for every day.
☐ I care for my friends.
☐ I can learn from my ancestors and my family.
☐ I can give up the need for approval of all my peers.
☐ I can do things for myself.

All of the choices above are correct. Most people check several. Furthermore, any of the statements above can begin helping you now, either alone or in combination with the techniques you will learn in the chapters that follow. When you finish reading a chapter, review this list. Realize that each statement is true in reality. Most of the statements are based on *Chazal.* Soon you will notice that these truisms are part of *your* life.

◢ I Wish I'd Known. . .

At the first session of our workshop, we tried to pinpoint when our lives started to become complicated. The group agreed that they first encountered difficult obstacles when they began high school. As Shira recalled, "We had a personal growth class with Rabbi Solomon once a week. One day he kept interrupting the discussion to make marks on the blackboard. After a while one of us asked what he was counting.

" 'This class has said the words, "I'm depressed" 105 times in the last half hour,' Rabbi Solomon replied."

I was surprised by the deep feelings that came up and the frustration that everyone shared. These issues were almost too painful to talk about then. Now, however, these young mothers know that they survived it all, and they may even wonder why they cared so much then.

You would never guess when you see these people today that they were once shy in high school. They rarely mention their fears and difficulties — from the mother who jogs into class in perfect shape to the prominent hostess, or the efficient mother of triplets and the energetic legal assistant. Each one is confident and self-assured. Here are a few of the feelings they shared. Each quote is from a different person.

● "I was the most unpopular kid in the class. I was the one who was never invited to parties."

● "I remember the extracurricular functions. If there was a *Melaveh Malkah,* play or choir, everyone went to try out but the teachers chose whomever they wanted."

- "I met someone at the reunion. She told me that when she went from eighth to ninth grade she was at an academic and social low. Suddenly in high school there was no time for asking questions. You took your notes and took your tests. She came into the school with a few close friends, but suddenly this year they didn't accept her in the same way as before."

- "I think the 'in-clique' had a nucleus of two or three girls and another six or seven girls floating on the outside hoping to get invited. For example, everyone was friendly with the good student before a test, but they wouldn't necessarily invite her on a *Chol HaMoed* outing."

If there was a magic pill you could take to make you popular and confident, would you take it? You probably would answer yes, without thinking twice. Popularity is probably a big goal for you right now. Sometimes it's even more important to you than good grades in school. Being part of the in-clique can certainly seem like the supreme goal. But will it really assure you joy and fulfillment?

Did you ever think that the popular girls have periods of insecurity too? Shaina recalled a conversation with a classmate in 11th grade that showed her that popular girls worry too.

- "I went to try out for the play in 11th grade. This really 'with-it' kid was just walking out. Her sister was heading the play. I looked at her and said, 'Why did you bother to try out?' She burst into tears. 'You don't know what it's like to be in my shoes. I often feel that my friends stay with me because of my last name, not for who I really am.' "

Some girls love competition. Most of us, however, wish that everyone could have a fair chance instead of the same girls doing things all the time while others are completely left out of school functions.

- "Those play tryouts were a horror. You had Tryouts 1 and Tryout 2. Then you had seven recalls. The tension, until the heads finally decided who to pick, gave me a stomach ache for two weeks!"

● "I felt awful when I wasn't accepted to be a C.I.T. in the camp I attended for four years. I felt it must mean that I'm not such a great person."

We also discussed how teachers can misunderstand our nervousness. Sometimes even when we do prepare, we just can't answer the questions because we feel so much pressure.

● "This teacher would call on me to read a *Rashi* and I could not do it. The pressure was immense. If you read the *Rashi* right, she would give you a good mark right away. If you hesitated while reading the *Rashi,* she'd start drilling you."

These comments refer to some of the problems we will be discussing in this book. If the struggle for independence, peer pressure, succeeding in school, or communication with parents and teachers is on your mind you'll find helpful ideas in the pages ahead.

However, please keep in mind that not every problem can be solved. Life isn't perfect. Remember though, even if you can't solve a specific problem, if you readjust your attitude and priorities you can still be a happier person.

❧ I Wish I'd Known

"What do you wish you had known then?" I asked the participants of the workshop.

● "I wish I'd known that this whole social issue will pass very quickly. Once everyone graduates from high school things become pretty evened out. The snobbiest girl in the class will live across the hall from you and you will be her best friend. You need an egg. She needs paprika. . ."

- "I wish I'd known that we should pay attention to *everything* about ourselves. You may not be a good student, yet you may have what it takes to cope really well in real life. A few weeks ago someone met me on the street and said, 'I didn't recognize you. I can't believe it. There were some girls who were such 'nebs' in school, then they get married and they are so put together.' She obviously didn't realize that she wasn't being especially tactful, but I decided to focus on my present success and not on the fact that I was once a 'neb.' "

- "I wish I'd known that it's not as important to have the whole class follow you as it is to have a few true friends. When our favorite eighth-grade teacher made a 10-year reunion in her home I knew I wouldn't miss it. I was curious to see who would make the effort to come back after all these years.

  "Not a single 'big-mouth' girl was there. The quiet girls came. The girls who always waited at the edge of the clique to be accepted came too. All the girls from my group came. We weren't the 'in-group' but we were really close and loyal to each other."

In many of the letters I receive, the same question comes up again and again, "What can I do to feel better about myself?" It's a mistake to think that self-confidence depends on whether or not others approve of you. You cannot control anyone but yourself. When you learn to spend time working on changing yourself instead of worrying about impressing others, you will have made an important discovery:

The number one key to success is not what others think of you but what you think of yourself.

Do you overlook your strengths and focus on your limitations? Do you concentrate on the negative or do you focus on the good that is happening to you? The Vilna Gaon says that it's human nature to take the good for granted, but the things that bother us are in the forefront of our mind. That's why we have so many opportunities to bless Hashem each day. The blessings remind us how fortunate we really are. In this book you will learn how to turn the negative thoughts around and how to build a system for feeling good about yourself.

If you practice the ideas in this book and think about some of them every day, you will not be disappointed!

✒ Quick Quiz

How Strong Are You Inside?

1. I blamed myself when I wasn't accepted to the camp I chose.
2. When I get a good mark I think it's more because of luck than because I deserved it.
3. When a girl from the "in-clique" is nice to me I feel suspicious.
4. The teachers listen to the girls who aren't afraid to talk back.
5. Tryouts aren't fair.
6. Giving others compliments about their talents makes me feel uncomfortable.
7. I don't ask questions in class because I'm afraid to sound stupid.
8. I will pass my classmate on the street without saying hello if she's not really my friend.
9. I didn't go to see the school's performance because I wasn't in it.
10. I like to impress people with the way I dress.
11. At choir practice, if someone's singing off-tune, it's me.
12. I find it difficult to continue once I've made a mistake.
13. I'm terrified of reading a *passuk* because I'll probably do it all wrong.
14. It's really hard for me to apologize.
15. I tend to get angry with my parents when something goes wrong with my friends.

Add up all your TRUE and FALSE statements.

TRUE _____ FALSE _____. If you scored over half of the items TRUE, you may want to spend some time thinking about why you have these feelings. If the majority of your answers were FALSE, you are on your way to greater happiness.

Dear Friends,

This book is a synthesis of the most practical and useful ideas I learned from the Torah and from hundreds of successful workshops with people like you.

A while back I met Yocheved and her mother. I hadn't seen Yocheved since I graduated from elementary school. "Are you the Roiza Weinreich who wrote the book about self-esteem?" the mother asked.

"Yes, I wrote *There Will Never Be Another You.* Did you like reading it?"

"Your book was amazing. I guess in order to write a book like that you must have always been confident. You must have been confident even as a child."

"I guess I must have. . .," I replied with a smile.

My thoughts travel back across the years. . .

I am standing in the school yard. They are picking *machanayim* teams. Yocheved is the captain of one of the teams. I stand there hoping that someone will pick me for their team. All the best girls are picked and I'm still standing near the gate. Please pick me . . . I'm so embarrassed, I plead inside. Finally there are only two of us left standing. I guess I really need to feel wanted . . . I'm not very good at dodging and I miss half the balls that are thrown to me. I hear my classmate's voice, "Look, we have to start the game. OK, I'll take Roiza and you'll take Shira."

Mrs. Z. and everyone else — I wasn't born absolutely confident. I didn't automatically have the courage to enjoy every new day, focus on the good and share a part of myself. Since those days of standing by the gate, I learned how to look for the good in myself and in others. I decided to write this book because it seemed like the best way to share the many wonderful things I have learned which have deepened my enjoyment of life.

If even one girl doesn't cry inside while she stands at the gate waiting . . . If even one girl finds the courage to accomplish the "impossible" . . . If even one girl learns how to enjoy life by reading this book . . . Then this book was a success.

One note: Each chapter has an exercise. Don't just skip over it. Do it! Think about it! That way you will see your life change.

Please write with your comments and suggestions. I will attempt to answer your letter. I really value your feedback.

This book is my present to you. Focus on the good. Enjoy every new day. Do all the little things well. Be the best you can be.

ENJOY THE BOOK!

Sincerely yours,

Roiza Weinreich

A Happier You

Chapter 1

> Our forefathers created a relationship with
> Hashem and we benefit from them. Avraham
> loved Hashem and was willing to defend
> Hashem's existence and honor against Nimrod
> . . . Avraham's love for Hashem later became
> an innate part of Jews for all generations
> never to be uprooted from them.
>
> Hashem promised Avraham that since he
> loved Hashem so much, Hashem would
> always love his Jewish descendants and they
> would always love Hashem. How does
> Hashem protect the love that the Jews have
> for Him? When we feel Hashem's love for us,
> then we also feel love for Hashem. Through
> this mirror-like process, Hashem protects the
> love . . . This idea is what is referred to in
> Yiddish as the "pintele Yid" — the indestruc-
> tible love that deep down we feel for Hashem.

(The Art Of Jewish Prayer, Rabbi Yitzchok Kirzner)

The Gift Inside Us

D o you have the same eyes as your mother or father?

Is your hair the same color as your aunt's hair?

Do people say you look just like another person in the family?

When I think about the topic of heredity, I remember the year I studied in Bais Yaakov in *Eretz Yisrael.* My roommate had a twin sister on the same floor. All the other twins I had met in my life were identical but Chany and Beily didn't look alike at all. I once asked Beily about it. Beily laughed, "It's been a wonder in my family for the past 18 years. I just don't look like either my mother or my father. Someone said I look like my great-aunt. I don't see any resemblance. Well, at least I know how I'll look when I'm 84."

It isn't only physical features that seem to run in families. We can also inherit talents such as a flair for drawing or an ear for music. Perhaps qualities and personality traits are part of your legacy. Some people are intellectual while others are emotional. Some people like to think things over while others make quick decisions. Even an approach to life might be inherited.

Were you named after a great-grandparent or another ancestor whom your parents admired? Do your parents ever say that you resemble the great-grandmother whom you were named after? Did you ever hear them comment, "You talk and move your hands just like your great-grandmother did. You have always been organized. Even when you were two years old you always put your toys away. Isn't it interesting? Your great-grandmother was organized too"?

❧ Understanding Heredity Gives Us Exceptional Inner Strength

Understanding heredity gives us exceptional inner strength.

Every *mitzvah* we do — from lighting Shabbos candles to sitting in the *succah* — has the force of the history of the Jewish nation in it. When we say *Az Yashir* in our prayers we are connecting with our ancestors who left Egypt thousands of years ago. Let's examine what heredity is and what it does for us.

Our Sages explain that heredity gives us a head start when we improve our personality. This is compared to a dwarf who couldn't see far and walked slowly. He met a giant and climbed on his shoulders. When he was on top of the giant's shoulders he could see farther and move quicker.

❧ Connecting With the Energy of Heredity

Like a dwarf on the shoulders of a giant, a person who climbs on his ancestor's shoulders will have a better likelihood of improving and going forward. You can plug into the energy of heredity by tuning in to your past. Each story and image in your past can help you progress. When you decide to pursue a goal you aren't alone, your ancestors are helping you succeed.

A common question that comes up at this point during the workshop is: "My grandfather isn't a *Rosh Yeshiva*, he's just an ordinary businessman. Do my grandparents have to be famous in order for me to inherit an extra edge?"

Don't be confused between using your lineage as a status symbol and knowing the inner strength that you have.

❧ Your Ancestors' Actions That Have Paved the Way for You

Even if your grandparents aren't famous, they have still done many wonderful *mitzvos* that have paved the way for you.

Each of us have very special people in our families. Our parents, grandparents, aunts and uncles have traits that we strive to follow. We derive from the Torah that מַעֲשֵׂה אָבוֹת סִימָן לַבָּנִים (*Tanchuma* 9:2; *Ramban, Lech Lecha* 12:6). This means that every good deed that Avraham, Yitzchak, Yaakov and Sarah, Rivkah, Rachel and Leah did makes it easier for every Jew to do those same good deeds. This principle applies as well to the actions of our own grandparents.

When we learn about the good deeds of the *Avos* and *Emahos,* with the awareness that they have paved the path for us, the concepts take on a new meaning.

❧ Drawing Water From the Wells

Reb Simcha Bunim of Otvosk became a Chassidic Rebbe at the age of seventeen. He visited Rav Yaakov Aryeh of Radziman and asked for a blessing on his new appointment.

Reb Yaakov Aryeh said, "I knew your grandfather well, and I hear about the great deeds of your father. Now what will be?"

Reb Simcha Bunim replied, "We see in the Torah that Avrahom dug wells and Yitzchak dug wells, but Yaakov didn't dig wells anymore. Since his father and grandfather dug the wells, the grandchild could go and get the water easily."

Reb Yaakov Aryeh smiled and gave the young Reb Simcha Bunim his blessings.

The deeds of our grandparents and parents planted a seed in us. We have inherited many wonderful traits. The values our parents and grandparents fought for are our inheritance. Now we only have to go over and draw the water from the wells of their good traits and good deeds.

Our ancestors' actions have made it easier for us to do the right thing. However, what we do with our gifts is still up to us. Even if it's easier, it doesn't happen by itself. We still have to decide to pursue the goal.

◢✺ Awareness: The First Step

The first step in easing our struggle to develop ourselves and to reap the benefit of our ancestor's actions is awareness. The voices of the *Avos* and *Emahos* down through the ages to our own parents and grandparents, are inside us. When we first listen to these voices we might not hear them clearly. We may be asleep and not hear these voices for a long interval. Then, suddenly we will be filled with energy and feel impatient, demanding more of ourselves than even our grandparents would. However if we give ourselves the opportunity to learn and grow gradually, we will see greater harmony in our personality.

> *A man once asked the Chofetz Chaim if he should write the true experiences and events in the life of his ancestors. He was afraid it might make him appear to be haughty.*
>
> *The Chofetz Chaim however told him to go ahead and he cited, to support his answer, a verse from the Written Torah: "Remember the days of old, understand the years of the many generations. Ask your father and he will inform you; your elders and they will tell you"* (Devarim 32:7).   (All for The Boss, Ruchoma Shain)

My oldest daughter, Chavie, is named after my grandmother. I believe that she is like her in many ways. I hope that she will inherit her great-grandmother's unique qualities when she grows up. I'm sure your parents have the same thoughts and prayers about each of you.

My grandmother felt that whenever possible you should give of yourself completely and do your best for others. She treated every person, even young children, with respect and warmth. I loved to talk to her because she would stop everything to hold my hand, look in my eyes and listen carefully to what I was saying. Her satisfaction stemmed from giving and therefore she was always happy.

On Purim Bubby was the queen of giving. She presided over a table overflowing with one hundred *mishloach manos* plates. Every friend, relative, neighbor and acquaintance stopped by. Everyone received a plate of her homemade cookies, rumballs, and other treats all beautifully wrapped. She knew what each person who visited was most interested in and made them feel welcome. I wonder now how she did it all!

Right after Purim, Bubby began cooking and baking for Pesach. She prepared packages of food that were distributed to hospitals through the *Bikur Cholim,* because at the time *Kosher L'Pesach* food was hard to find in the hospital.

I don't know when Bubby learned English. She arrived in the United States after World War II at the age of 57. She spoke English fluently and read quite a lot. She could write in English but she sometimes had trouble with spelling. Nevertheless, she sent me letters when I was in camp that I still have today. After all, if I wrote to her she had to write back and she knew I'd enjoy getting mail in camp.

You need a large measure of discipline and determination if you are to overcome the obstacles of old age. A person with discipline exerts themselves to set goals every day and achieve them. Bubby always had something constructive to accomplish and she proceeded even if she didn't feel well.

Bubby had a schedule. Every day began with cooking and while the food cooked, she straightened up the house. Then each day had its special project. On Monday she sewed, on

Tuesday she baked, on Wednesday she shopped and did errands, and on Thursday she prepared for Shabbos so that on Friday she could welcome Shabbos without a rush.

I remember going to *shul* with her on Shabbos. Everyone rushed over to greet her. She had a smile and a wise word for everyone. She never complained, but rather looked for the good in everyone. She took the time to thank people for the slightest favor.

Learning How to Live

From books we gain knowledge, but from people we learn how to live. The knowledge that we learn from books is limited. It helps us build skills and teaches us important information. Learning life skills is much more vital. Every little detail you pick up from those closest to you about how to act and how to speak and how to overcome obstacles can be applied in thousands of situations.

There is an entire world under the ocean that we cannot see if we look only at the surface water. There are diamonds and gold hidden in the earth. There are probably some of your personal treasures under the bed or in the bottom of your closet. If you don't look you will not find them.

Likewise the qualities of someone close to you are hidden under the layers of routine life. The Tiferes Shmuel once said, "My father once gave me the portion of *afikoman* and said, '*Tzafun,* hide it.' Perhaps he was alluding to the verse 'I have hidden Your word in my heart that I might not sin,' (*Tehillim* 119: 11)." Searching for the *afikoman* reminds us that we have to look for the unacknowledged achievements of our elders and store them away deep inside our heart.

Don't let the uniqueness of the individual become lost because there are too many things you have to see and do. Do you find that you don't have time to make meaningful contact with your relatives? No time to watch your mother as she handles a difficult situation because you have a test tomorrow? No time to join your older sister in saying *Tehillim* because you'll be late for your appointment? No time to listen to your father's *Dvar Torah* because your friends came early to pick you up? Sometimes we will sit for an hour and listen to a stranger and be so impressed while we have barely glanced at the qualities of those closest to us.

∝ Do You Want to Know —

● What obstacles have your parents overcome and how?

● How does your aunt who suffers from arthritis find strength and comfort?

● What does your grandmother like to do?

● When is your great-uncle happy?

Take a moment now to think about your parents and ancestors. How are they unique? How do you want to be like them? Make an appointment to talk to your relatives and ask them for ideas and advice.

∝ Feeling Comfortable When Talking. . .

The main thing to remember about good conversation is that both people should do some listening as well as some talking. If you follow the advice in *Pirkei Avos* that a wise person learns from everyone, your conversations will improve.

When you called a friend yesterday and talked about the school assembly you had a conversation. When you are talking about a pleasant subject the conversation is usually easy for everyone. When you disagree with someone it's more complex to keep the lines of communication open.

Your tone of voice can make a big difference in how people will react. If you state ideas in a loud voice, people might think you want to argue even if you don't mean it that way. Don't be afraid to ask questions; however, speak in a soft but confident voice.

What your questions should *not* be:

A. Too personal — My 2-year-old asked a balding relative why his hair was is so thin. It was cute for a 2-year-old but older people shouldn't ask personal questions.

B. Unpleasant subjects — If you know that mentioning a certain topic like an accident or bad news will upset the person you are approaching, talk about something else.

C. Me, Me, Me! — We can't learn much and we become pretty boring if we speak about ourselves all the time.

From Ideas to Real Life

On some occasions following in our parents' footsteps is easy. If we see our parents model a specific trait often, it becomes a part of us without our even realizing that it happened. We have thousands and thousands of impressions, some originating in childhood, others derived from more recent experiences. In many areas you are ready right now to act properly without conscious effort.

If you discover new qualities you weren't aware of until now, you might need to plan how you will incorporate these new ideas into your life. Even that isn't so difficult. Just apply yourself, be determined and give yourself a chance. Yes, it takes effort and your first attempt might not be perfect. But if you follow the steps outlined in this book you will see your life change.

Everyone can.

Exercise

מָתַי יַגִּיעוּ מַעֲשַׂי לְמַעֲשֵׂי אֲבוֹתַי — In what way can I be a little bit like. . .

I learned that . . .

1. _____

from. . .

_____

I learned that. . .

2. _____

from. . .

_____

Actual Responses
Learning from Relatives

I learned how to welcome guests,

   from my grandmother. Whenever I come to visit her for Shabbos, she asks what my favorite foods are so that she can prepare them for me. She also takes me out on Sunday and buys me a special treat.

Chavie W.

I learned to make fresh *challah* in honor of Shabbos,

   from my mother. Every week my mother makes *challah* on Thursday. She prepares the dough while we are in school but she saves a piece of dough for each of us so that we can braid a *challah* of our own.

I learned how to have fun on rainy days,

   from my great-aunt. We visited her on a rainy day and

she had so many great things for us to do. First we had a scavenger hunt around her house. She has the most interesting things in her house. Afterwards we made big collage pictures out of ribbon, *Shanah Tovah* cards and old buttons that she was probably saving for 10 years.   *Chaya Rivka W.*

I learned to do *chesed* for others,

from my mother. She sends money to tons of charities and volunteers to make sick people very happy. She is in charge of the Chanukah campaign for the Yeshiva. She sits for hours stuffing envelopes with order forms and then she walks around the whole school giving them out. She sits for hours counting the money and organizing the orders. Then she packs bags and boxes full of oil, candles and wicks. She helps with so many affairs, to set up and prepare food, etc. I could go on and on.   *Elky B.*

I learned that for Shabbos you buy the nicest,

from my parents. My mother prepares all the delicacies, like the sweet-and-sour salmon, chopped liver and fruit platters featuring out-of-season fruits. My father makes sure to have food that the children will especially enjoy, things like *nosh,* seven-layer cake and salami.

I learned to take time to listen to little kids,

from my uncle. Whenever the family gets together for a *Melaveh Malkah* or a Chanukah party he walks over to each of the young cousins and spends a few minutes talking to them.   *Blima Gitty F.*

I learned sincere faith,

from my *bubby.* Every Shabbos afternoon she's bent over her worn-out *Tehillim,* conducting a silent dialogue with Hashem. She looks like she is talking to an intimate friend who will grant everything graciously.

When I watch my precious *bubby* bent over her *Tehillim,* this scenario revolves in my mind. She came to America after surviving a curtain of darkness, she showed a tough determination and intense desire to justify the fact that Hashem had chosen her to live. My *bubby* and *zeidy* slowly and surely managed not only to survive as new immigrants but to help others do the same.   *Raizy Z.*

I learned that you should respect and care for parents,

from my grandparents. They take care of my great-grandmother, who has a room and kitchen in their house. She is part of the family and yet she still has independence and dignity.   *Devorah S.*

I learned that one can balance a life of Torah learning and work,

from my father. Every morning he wakes up between 4:30 and 5:00 to learn before his long day at work.
Tziri F.

I learned that in life what matters is that you try hard and persevere. If things don't work out, it's for the best,

from my mother. My mother has encouraged me in this way very often because many times I try out for plays and my mother always tells me, "Don't be disappointed if you don't get a certain part. Something else good will come soon. You'll see."   *Malky T.*

I learned to do a *mitzvah* even if it means overcoming obstacles,

from my grandparents. First my grandparents lived in Syracuse, but my grandfather kept losing his job every week because he didn't want to work on Shabbos. Then in Reading, Pennsylvania my grandfather got a job sewing army uniforms. In this job he didn't have to work on Shabbos. Even though there were very few Jews there, they moved to Reading because he didn't have to work on Shabbos. When he lost that job, they moved to Rochester. In Rochester my grandparents opened their own cleaning and tailoring store. But even though they had their own store, it was still hard. A lot of people wanted to pick up or bring in clothing on Shabbos.   *Chaya W.*

I learned how to find the courage to go on in life when my grandmother was *niftar,*

from my mother. She told me the following parable:

> *With the last blast of the horn, the ship set sail. Mother and daughter were seen waving until the ship left beyond the horizon. The tearful goodbyes were eased when a reassuring thought came to mind. Here we are waving goodbye while on the other side there are many more people waving hello. We cry over the departure while others are happy over the arrival.*

After someone is *niftar,* we cry. That person left this world, but a reassuring thought comes to mind. There in the World of Truth people are happy because they are finally reunited. My grandparents led a fulfilling life together, helping everyone in need. Now again they are together, sharing their place in *Olam Haba.*   *Shaindy J.*

I learned to love doing useful, creative activities in order to relax,

from my grandmother. My grandmother loves to sew. Whenever she has a spare moment she sits down by her sewing machine and starts working on something. She says it helps her relax. Occasionally when my mother and I go shopping for an outfit, we can't find anything we like. When we come home we call my grandmother and ask her if she has time to make me an outfit. When it's done you can't tell it was homemade.   *Chaya Perel W.*

I learned that focusing on others gives you strength,

from my aunt. My aunt has arthritis. It's hard for her to get around. But when we visit she feels revived. She finds strength when we, her great-nieces, come to visit her. She enjoys our company and gets up and hobbles around bringing things she thinks we'd enjoy.   *Perel R.*

I learned that "Old age is only in the mind. If you don't mind, then you are not old,"

from my grandmother. That's my grandmother's favor-ite saying. She's the funniest and most loving grand-mother. She loves to go shopping at Loeh-manns, take walks in the park and go to Torah lec-tures once a week. In her apartment, my grand-mother listens to Torah tapes while she cleans. My grandmother stays young by keeping busy.

I learned to be happy with life,

from my parents. Their obstacle in life was that both of my parents didn't have parents to help them or sup-port them financially, physically and emotionally. They give all seven of us a happy wonderful home.

I learned faith in Hashem,

from my aunt. Although she went through a few major operations, she didn't panic and was able to have full faith in Hashem that things will be fine. Because of this she has merited to see 10 grand-children, thank G-d.   *Chanie F.*

I learned to be happy with my home,

from my mother. My mother had surgery this past week and she's still overcoming the pain. When she sees us at her bed every morning with her breakfast, she smiles and says,"It's good to be home." *Rifky*

2-Minute Tips

1. **Have Courage**
   Visualize the end, then construct the means. Tell yourself that you are MORE than able. Imagine that through this conversation you will learn more about yourself and those closest to you and it will even help you deal with difficulties in your relationships.

2. **Advice on Neutral Topics**
   Ask for advice from your relatives. Start by asking about neutral topics — such as a good cookie recipe or help in putting together a matching outfit. As your confidence and your close feeling grow you'll feel more comfortable about opening up.

3. **Share a Part of Yourself**
   Share what you experience. Call someone you admire and tell them something you learned or something you are proud of. If your relatives live far away, write a letter.

4. **How Is Your Family Alike?**
   Find three things you have in common with one of your parents.

Now I Know!

- Every family has a special legacy.

- Heredity is the gift inside us that gives us inner strength.

- The traits, speech and deeds of our grandparents and parents planted a seed in us. Their actions have made it easier for us to do the right thing.

- The uniqueness of your parents and relatives need not get lost in the everyday routine of life. Set aside an hour to talk with your relatives and learn from them.

Chapter 2

" *I woke up one morning feeling bright and gay,*
There really was no reason
on this ordinary day.
But something inside me said,
"Be happy today,"
And smile at everyone that comes your way.

For a moment or two I sat pondering,
How did this idea enter my mind?
Maybe I should just ignore it
and leave it behind.

But that something inside me was at it again,
It told me, "Be joyous and glad" just then.
So I obeyed right on the spot,
I didn't know why, I just said, "Why not?"

A good mood can't hurt anyone,
It can just make life more fun.
I should be full of appreciation
To everyone in Hashem's creation.

So I told the voice inside me
As quickly as can be,
You are more than welcome any day
For You have shown me the true way. "

(Gitty Malky Braun)

Happiness on Ordinary Days

*M*y grandmother had many wonderful talents, feelings and characteristics. There is one trait that I hope Chavie inherits from her *bubby* when she grows up, because it can change her life. No matter what life brings, that one quality can always help her. I hope that as she matures, she will love every day of life because she hopes to do her best with it.

I'm Happy I've Lived to See This Day

It was a Sunday night I never forgot. I was seven years old and my sister Manya was getting married. Bubby was riding with us to the wedding hall. I ran upstairs to get something from my room. Bubby was in my parents' bedroom checking her *sheitel* and putting on her jewelry. I knocked. I wanted to show

Bubby my hair. I had been at the hairdresser's for two hours that afternoon. My hair was in bottle curls. I had never felt so glamorous. Bubby called, "Come in." I saw her reflection in the mirror before she turned around. Bubby looked so beautiful. The blonde *sheitel* (Bubby never wore a gray *sheitel* — not even when she was 89) looked perfect. Everything matched.

My *bubby* made her own style. The dress . . . I knew she had sewn the dress herself. She made most of the clothes she wore because she didn't like what they had in the stores. Everything was of a very fine quality. She always wore a brooch and earrings. She never wore orthopedic shoes.

She turned away from the mirror and I saw tears in her eyes. Bubby crying! I was shocked. I had never seen Bubby cry. I was confused. Today is a happy day.

"Bubby, why are you crying? What's wrong?" I asked.

"My child, I'm not crying because I'm sad. I'm crying because I'm happy. This is the first time in my life that I will be at the wedding of a grandchild. I'm happy I've lived to see this day. I pray to Hashem to be at the wedding of another grandchild too." And then there were tears in Bubby's eyes again.

"Bubby, don't worry!" I exclaimed. "I'm sure you'll be at the weddings of all five of us and I'll dance with you at my wedding too."

Why should Bubby worry? Bubby was young. She always stood straight and tall. She was as active and energetic as my mother. Wouldn't Bubby live forever?

Bubby knew that she was 84 years old so she didn't answer. She just gathered me in her arms and hugged me tight and smiled a small smile. That warm, comfortable feeling made me happy as I ran down the stairs to wait for my sister, the *kallah,* to come down.

✎ There's an Opportunity for Something Good Every Day

Actually I had heard Bubby say, "I'm happy I've lived to see this day," on many "ordinary" days. I remember walking with

Bubby to buy some groceries. I think I was in the second grade, and Bubby was 81. I marveled at her quick determined stride. I could barely keep up with her. We had just turned the corner of 50th Street when Bubby met a friend her age. The friend however walked slowly and was bent over. She grumbled to herself as she walked.

"How do you still walk quickly and with perfect posture?" I asked my grandmother. Perhaps Bubby knew about osteoporosis, but she didn't think I'd understand that, so she explained, "Of course it's a gift from Hashem, but attitude helps. If you walk around feeling that life is a burden, you'll become a hunchback before you know it. Life is a precious gift and there is always an opportunity for something good every day."

Bubby's soul overflowed with the pure joy of being alive. She was determined to live life to the fullest. She might have felt stiff but she didn't stay home. She was determined to live even when she didn't feel well. A picture of her when she was 88, visiting me in sleepaway camp, reminds me of this fact. She is still standing tall but she is leaning just a little against the tree. I remember that during that visit when she walked, she leaned on my arm a little. She had been having dizzy spells, but refused to get a cane. When she went out in the city she used her shopping cart for balance. The fact that she didn't travel well in cars didn't stop her from coming to visit me in camp. Bubby retained a young person's energy and excitement until she breathed her last breath. She walked through life with her eyes wide open, not half shut. She felt that "whichever way life turns out it, is the best way for me because I can always do something good."

⚞ Attitude

Do you have younger siblings who bounce out of bed with smiles each morning? In 10 minutes they are running to wake up everyone in the house and insisting that they be fully dressed from hat to shoes. After 15 minutes they ask to go "Bye-Bye."

Babies have positive expectations of themselves and of their world. When infants begin to crawl they really push themselves. They constantly scramble and climb as they explore and look for new things. They aren't worried about falling — when they fall they get right up again and continue their search. On the other hand every new discovery brings a cry of joy.

That inner spark is something we all had as young children. However when we start school and are often criticized, we lose our innocent joy. We can reignite that inner spark of enthusiasm now. It just takes concentration and effort.

> At times life can appear to be gray and gloomy, boring in its seeming repetition. Life becomes full of flavor and meaning only after a person looks at it with great love, if he sees every occurrence as an opportunity to give and to fulfill the Divine Will.   (Rav Yitzchak Ariel)

Life is not what happens to you but how you look at it. We tend to sit back and expect the flavor and joy in life to come from things that happen to us. Rav Yitzchak Ariel explains that the flavor and joy comes not from things outside us but from in our hearts.

Spend a few minutes every morning thinking about the day ahead. Look at how you can make each part of your day a little better. Make an effort to eliminate any worries. As you begin to see your family and later your friends, greet them with a smile. Soon you will have more friends. People will look for you in the morning because they will know you will greet them with a smile.

The following story describes Chedva Silberfarb in her teenage years. Chedva A"H always had a talent for turning a difficult situation into something positive. As an adult she amazed everyone who knew her with her optimistic view of life. She dedicated her life to speaking of the importance of "Shemiras Halashon" to thousands of people.

ᨀ We Both Had a Ball
Preparing a Day of Fun for You

A blustery cold winter day in Yerushalayim. Any minute torrents of rain will fall. Chedva checks her watch. The girls in her Shabbos group are supposed to meet her here in a few minutes for an outdoor day of fun. Will anyone brave the elements today? Chedva arrives at the designated meeting place and meets one of her charges.

Chedva says, "I have a great activity planned for you today." Running to catch up with Chedva, the young girl wonders what Chedva has in store for her. In a few moments, they have arrived at Chedva's house. Chedva rolls up her sleeves, turns on a musical tape, gathers cleaning equipment and attacks the household chores with great vigor. Her young friend joins in the fun, and with great enthusiasm they clean up the entire house. Mrs. Angel returns home to a spotless house. She teases Chedva, "Nu, did you have a day of fun today with your girls?"

"Yes, we both had a ball, preparing a day of fun FOR YOU!" (*A Narrow Bridge*)

To keep your positive morning attitude strong throughout the day, make an "attitude check" before each meal. Take a minute to ask yourself how you feel. Did you get tense without realizing it ?

ᨀ Attitude Check

1. What word would I use to describe my emotions right now?

Happy? Sad? Angry? Worried? Bored? _____

2. What's the best thing that happened to me today?

_____

3. What's the worst thing that happened to me today?

   _____

4. Which event has affected me more, the good or the bad ?

   _____

What happens if you've checked how you are feeling and you realize you are feeling a little down right now? Look for a way to change things. It may be as simple as taking a few deep breaths, closing your eyes and picturing the good things that have happened to you so far. You can take a short walk, talk to a friend or suck your favorite candy.

A sense of humor helps loads. Here's how one girl found something to be thankful for in going to school, everyone's least favorite occupation!

Hooray for School!
Raizy G.

One very cold morning when it wasn't sunny,
I woke up feeling very funny.
Not only did my head ache and my feet feel sore,
I felt very tired, what a day I had in store!

Then I was told by the doctor that I had the flu.
Hurray! I didn't have to go to school!

The first week at home was a great success,
All I did all day was rest.

The second week that I stayed at home
I began to feel sad and very alone.
It became a terrible bore
and I waited for my friends to come and visit me more.

Finally I was better and the doctor said,
I wouldn't be so bored because I'd be out of bed.
Boy, was I happy and feeling all right,
I'd see all my friends, what a delight!

The next day I woke up early and bright,
I got all dressed and packed myself up.
After quickly eating some breakfast food,
I ran out to school in a very good mood.

I never really felt happy about learning,
I had always thought that it was boring.
My hands once again from my pen are all inky,
Thank you Hashem for changing how I think.

If none of these ideas work, remember a person, place, or event from your life that makes you feel uplifted. Create a personal happy place with your imagination. Your "happy place" should be a personal memory that brings a smile to your face. Think of something specific.

One way we can rejoice is to contemplate how much joy we give to Hashem, each of us in our unique way. R' Moshe Leib of Sassov once said, "The Torah tells us that Hashem 'passed over the houses of the *Yidden* in Egypt.' Are we to take this in a literal sense? How can we? His glory fills the entire world. We must rather imagine that when Hashem came upon the home of a *Yid* living in an Egyptian neighborhood, He would 'skip and dance,' so to speak, and say with joy, 'A Jew lives here! A Jew lives here!' "

I always smile when — as you may have guessed — I think of my grandmother.

✎ Many "Impossible" Things Can Be Accomplished if You Try

Bubby patiently taught me many of the skills I needed for growing up. She didn't grimace when you made a mistake and would smile as she showed you how to do things correctly.

There is a little gray sweater I have that reminds me of one of the most wonderful ideas on living life to the fullest that I've learned from Bubby, so read carefully. This concept helped me write my books and accomplish many other things despite doubts and fear.

Bubby taught me that my dreams aren't just an illusion. If I really try, many "impossible" things can be accomplished.

I have a treasure that represents Bubby's attitude. It's a child's size-three sweater that she knitted for me. I remember how she sat and played with me under a tree. Casually, she asked, "I want to make you a sweater and I want it to be something you like. What color do you want it to be?"

I opened my arms wide and said childishly,"I want my sweater to be every color — red, blue, green, pink, gray, yellow and orange." Even as I recited the list I felt a doubt creep in. No one has a sweater with every color. It's an impossible request.

My grandmother smiled and nodded to herself. I think she was proud that I could name so many colors. We continued to play and I forgot about the sweater, but Bubby didn't forget.

Three months later, I got the sweater of my dreams. It has a gray border and the middle has stripes of every color I named. She must have used all the scraps in her yarn bag to make it. The sweater taught me the important lesson that many things that seem impossible at first *can* be accomplished with thought, determination and caring.

I still have that sweater and just holding it in my hands makes me feel good.

Every part of Bubby's personality can help Chavie. A talent for writing can help her write letters and compositions, or a talent for art and doing crafts can help her put together beautiful things. But if Chavie inherits this positive attitude from Bubby — the pure joy of being alive — it will change the way she handles every day of her life. Her life will be full of possibilities instead of obstacles.

The decision to be happy even on ordinary days is the first step. "Don't wait for special days to feel good. There is no such thing as the right time, only the present time. The present time can be made into the perfect time. No matter what is happening, the biggest influence on any moment is your actions. It is your choices and your actions that make the perfect moment for you" (*Willpower,* Linda Stephens).

Your attitude really can change your life. However, there are a few simple things you can do to bring happiness into your life. I feel that there are three important steps that help a person enjoy life. These three things are like rungs on a ladder. When we do them we climb up towards happiness. I learned these three things from Bubby even after she passed away.

A. Plan Ahead

My grandmother passed away in 1976 and I got married in 1982, but I have a needlepoint hanging in my dining room that she made as a wedding gift for me. She prepared a needlepoint for each grandchild to be presented on their wedding day, wrapped it carefully and put it in a special drawer.

My needlepoint is a picture of a vase of roses. Perhaps because my name is Roiza?

B. Be Prepared

Bubby wasn't the type who woke up on Friday morning to make potato *kugel* and then discovered that there were no potatoes. She had a system. Putting your life in order seems like a lot of hard work, but it's a skill that can be learned. It's important to be prepared if you want to do things the right way and enjoy life fully.

Being prepared can save you from hassles every day. It could even save your life. Perhaps you were never stuck in the desert without water. However, were you ever lost and couldn't make a phone call because you didn't have a quarter? Did you ever panic before a test because you didn't have a pen or pencil? Have you ever lost an important letter before you mailed it because you didn't have a stamp handy? Did you ever take twenty pictures before you realized that there was no film in your camera? If you use your knowledge to plan ahead you can make your important times successful and hassle free.

After Bubby passed away, we gave away her old clothes. Before we packed a raincoat into the box, I put my hand in the pocket and pulled out a silk scarf. I smiled through my tears. Bubby always had a matching scarf ready in the pocket of each coat. I couldn't use the raincoat because Bubby was about 8 inches taller than I, but I still have the scarf 16 years later.

It's important to have all the little essentials under control because the reward is peace of mind. It's the simple secret of those who consistently do things well.

✎ C. You Can Always Help

I was packing to go home from the bungalow colony. There were six bulky items that wouldn't fit into our car. I asked around for someone who was renting a van or truck to take those items back to the city for me. After using up all the extra space in my friends' vehicles, I approached the people in the colony that I didn't know well — I was desperate. One woman stopped me and said, "You look familiar, what was your maiden name?"

"My name was Perlman."

"Was your grandmother Chava Perlman?"

"Yes," I replied.

"Well, I guess I recognize you from the times you visited her. I'll make room for your lawn chair. I'll be glad to repay a favor. I was your grandmother's downstairs neighbor. I'll never forget how helpful she was. Whenever she saw me with the baby carriage she would put down her shopping bag and rush to help me with the carriage. 'I have to help you, I know how hard it is to go up these steps with the baby and the carriage by yourself,' she would say with a smile."

Bubby divided her shopping and made lists because the doctor had told her that she shouldn't carry heavy bundles. Yet she would put her little bundle down and rush to help the neighbor with the heavier carriage.

Update how you look at life. Replace complaints with thoughtful and kind words. Everyone looks prettier with a smile on her face.

Why do we sample a new shampoo or a new skin lotion? We hope it will improve our looks. Yet the directions on almost every shampoo and skin lotion say that it takes two or three weeks before you notice a difference. If it takes time just to change how we look on the outside, it surely takes time to change how we look at life.

✍ Interview

People who study personalities say that there are two types of people. Some people are "wave riders," others are "wave fighters." A wave rider can be swimming in the stormiest ocean yet still manage to stay on top. A wave fighter might be swimming in a calm lake but gets scared anyway and begins thrashing so much that he feels that he is going to drown.

Kaila is definitely a wave rider. She is a master at staying on course and keeping her perspective when things go wrong. At work I've never seen her speak with impatience to an inept assistant and when I call her at home she manages to handle numerous interruptions without losing her composure. Several years ago we had to enter the *shul* to set up for a *tzedakah* function and when we arrived at the door with all the food, we realized that the key didn't work. Everyone was tense and edgy but Kaila kept calm. She saved the day when she thought of asking a neighbor for help. The neighbor opened the door for us.

I decided to ask Kaila for her ideas on dealing with the problems in life.

Roiza: When did you face a problem that worried you a lot in the past five years ?

Kaila: When we bought our home we had many unexpected

expenses. We did repairs in the house and they cost us about 20 percent more than expected. We had to dip into our savings more than once to cover the bills. About a week before the moving date I realized that we didn't have enough money in the bank to pay the movers.

Roiza: So you had to obtain several hundred dollars in a week. What options did you have for securing the money you needed ?

Kaila: We could have asked my parents or parents-in-law for the money. However there were problems with that option. I didn't feel comfortable explaining how tight our finances actually were. They would probably reproach us for spending more than we could afford and getting into this mess. I felt so embarrassed that I asked my husband to do the borrowing.

Roiza: I guess you felt that although it wasn't ideal to borrow, you didn't have another choice. Is that how you solved the problem?

Kaila: Actually, we never did borrow the money. On the night before our move I realized that neither my parents or in-laws had spoken to me about overspending so I concluded that my husband had not followed my suggestion. I said, "The movers are coming tomorrow morning. Now it's too late to borrow. How will we pay them?" My husband said, "Don't worry."

Roiza: How did you feel? Did you worry?

Kaila: Of course I worried. I've always taken my responsibilities seriously. My husband's a dentist and we've always met our bills. I felt very uneasy having people come and not having the money for them. My husband was amazing. He was really calm. The next morning when the movers came I whispered to him, "The movers are here. How will we pay?" He answered, "Hashem will help, don't worry." I got really involved in supervising the move after that and I couldn't think of anything else for several hours. Finally the movers finished unloading the truckload of furniture and appliances in our new home. My husband walked over to them with a smile and handed them the full $900 in cash.

Roiza: You must have been surprised.

Kaila: I sure was. I was so surprised and elated that I didn't even think of asking how he got the money. My husband smiled after the movers left and said, "Well don't you want to know where I got the money? A check came from the I.R.S. in today's mail. It was almost to the penny what we needed. When I cashed the check I had $6 change. I told you that Hashem would help us."

Roiza: What did you learn from this?

Kaila: I have quoted this story to my children so many times when we've had problems, both minor and major, that it is a family classic. Hashem is helping all of us all the time. These minor miracles frequently happen for those who **trust in Hashem.** Because of their trust they **notice Hashem's guidance** while others are too busy complaining to see how the Creator provides.

Exercise

When something is brand new we easily focus on its advantages and it gives us a lot of pleasure. After we have it for a while we start to take it for granted and even complain about it. As a first step to enjoying every day of life let's enjoy all the little things that we have around us.

Close your eyes for a few minutes. Now open your eyes and look around you. Pretend you have never seen any of the things before. Look at everything as if you were born today and are now seeing it for the first time.

_____

_____

_____

Actual Responses

Gratitude

(Note: Some of the responses are majestic; others discuss very ordinary everyday things like telephones. I left in the ordinary examples because this is your book and the responses should reflect what you feel.)

Me. I am. I see. I hear.
I have hands. I have feet.
What can I do with all these?

I have a mouth.
I open and close it, I wonder —
So many teeth. A tongue, lips.
There is a mirror.
I guess that must be me.
I like me.

This room. What's in it?
There are drawers to explore.
A closet of treasures.
There are books on the shelves.
What's in them?
There is a telephone.
How does it work?
What is it for?

It's comfortable in here.
Why is it warm?
There are windows. I look outside.
There is so much outside.
A sky, a sidewalk, other houses . . .
Who lives there?

There is a baby.
He smiles at me. I feel happy.

I smile back at him. He waves.
I wave back.

I see a thing on the wall.
I try it.
Suddenly
the room is flooded with light.
This is fun!
I touch the switch again
It is dark.
I touch the switch once more.
Light! It's marvelous.
So easy! How?

I open the closet.
It is full of different
things to wear.
Do they fit me?
It will be fun to try them on.
So many things.
Dresses, tops, skirts.
Look at this.
Ten pairs of shoes.
Are they my size too?
Everything is so colorful.

Someone wanted me
to be happy.

I open my eyes to an exotic sight. Hey, there's a tree with dark green leaves. Look there's a flower covered with bees. There up in the sky, the pale morning moon and down on this earth, a black racoon. Blue and white clouds way up in the sky, and beautiful red roses say hi! The bright yellow sun, shining in my eyes, and the still green grass, there it lies. The pink tulip, swaying to and fro, and that shrinking yellow daisy, trying hard to grow. I look up and see the little birds rest, in the nest other birds rest. They chirp and sing their morning melody. They wake up the world, using all their energy.

People whiz by as they rush to work. The bus driver is honking and going berserk.

Today I stopped to look. I opened my eyes. For all these creations, I must be so grateful.   *Devorah S.*

The World and Its Colors
Miriam Dina A.

The world is nice and beautiful,
With trees and grass and flowers.
There are so many colors,
Red, orange, green and blue,
Pink, black, brown and golden yellow too.

Hashem made the sky and the sun by day,
And at night the stars and moon play
The tune of:
Mah Rabu Maasecha Hashem.

Let's look at the wonders of Hashem,
Let's take five minutes of the day
To think and write about
Mah Rabu Maasecha Hashem.

Those minutes are valuable,
We can merit Olam Haba through them.
Please, everyone!
I beg of you!
Please think about Mah Rabu Maasecha Hashem.
It will brighten up your day!

I walked over to the window and looked outside. I saw the sky. Wow! I hadn't realized how late it was. The sun was setting. I saw orange, yellow, pink, purple and blue.

Then I saw my garden, full of flowers, grass, bushes and trees. There were pretty tulips and daffodils. I liked how they looked against the background of dark green bushes. As I turned away I thanked Hashem. *Bracha Leah D.*

I thank Hashem for all the things I have. Hashem gives people sisters and brothers to help each other. Hashem gives a house to my family so we don't have to stay outside. We also have food to eat and money to buy things and to give to *tzedakah*. Hashem gives us hands to write things down so we don't have to memorize everything. We can also make things with our hands. Hashem gives us feet to walk, to dance and to run. Hashem give us teachers to make arts and crafts with us, to play games and other things. Hashem gives us a voice to talk, to sing and we don't have to use motions when we have something to say. Thank you, Hashem, a lot. *Leah Malka G.*

Thank you, Hashem, for electrical devices. Our clock tells us what time it is. We know when it's time to *daven* and when it's time to do other *mitzvos*. Our washing machine gives us clean clothes. What would we do without electrical devices?

Rivka L.

שֶׁעָשָׂה לִי כָּל צָרְכִּי
Thank you, Hashem. You give me all my needs.

I wake up every morning and the sun shines through my room. Without even opening the light there is so much light in my room. I thank Hashem that I have such nice clothing. Some people aren't as fortunate as I am. When I come downstairs there is cereal, milk, orange juice and eggs. I make sure to eat every bit of it because some people are hungry and if I waste food it's like I don't care. Then I go off to school and learn many things. In some countries it's forbidden to learn any

Jewish things or to be a religious Jew. Then comes recess! I see the beautiful trees in the yard outside. Thank you, Hashem, for the wonderful things You make and do! *Ruchoma L.*

Heaven is a place on earth. It begins Friday night when my mother lights the *Shabbos licht*. I smell the wonderful home-made *challah,* fish, chicken, *kugel* and all the wonderful things my mother cooks in honor of this heavenly day. It feels as if we can touch the sky and bring heaven down to earth.

As I set the table I think, "I don't have anything to worry about tomorrow." I think of the *zemiros* my father will sing that lift my spirits high with pride, the *parshah* questions and my beautiful *Dvar Torah*. When I'm finished setting the table I think of my wonderful father, mother, brother, sister and my friends. Singing, laughing, treats and friends make Shabbos even more special. We feel as if heaven is on earth. *Rivky B.*

I stood there listening. I heard a sweet "chirp-chirp." I curiously but timidly walked closer to investigate. I saw the most beautiful and attractive little bird. How gracefully and lightly it glided across the blue of the sky. What an amazing creation of Hashem ! It's beautiful and flies so gracefully. It's incredible. *Sarala Z.*

I am lying comfortably under my warm down quilt on a freezing cold December night. How would things be if I would be outside now? I would be shivering to pieces. I would be terribly frightened in the pitch-black darkness of the night. But I open my eyes, and I'm inside, under my warm quilt in my familiar comfortable bedroom. Yet living in this spacious house, I am always complaining. Although I do have things to complain about, I am *Baruch Hashem* living in a house. *Miriam S.*

When our fridge broke this past Shabbos I realized how important it is. We didn't have any cold drinks or any dairy products or anything. A lot of food spoiled. The meat in our freezer got soft. The ice-cream cake melted. The ice became water. Our family went on a diet — instead of soda we drank regular tap water, not ice cold since we had no ice.

Now that our fridge is broken, I realize how grateful I should be when it works. I can't just open the fridge, stand there for a few minutes with the door open, and decide what treat I want to eat.

Chanie F.

A New Day
Rivka Berger

A brand new day is starting,
The sun comes out and the moon is parting.

We open our eyes. "Modeh Ani" we say,
Thank you, Hashem, for another bright day!

We thank Hashem for our body with so many parts,
First of all we thank Him for our heart.

We have a heart which to live we need,
Two eyes Hashem gave us with which we can read.

On each side of our face, we have an ear
So that every day, good news we can hear.

We have two feet, so we can walk,
And a mouth on our face to talk.

We have a nose, so we can smell,
And fingers to hold things very well!

And most of all our Neshamah so we can live,
And a feeling of kindness, so we can give!

So in short, we thank Hashem
For every limb in our body, every one of them!

Peace
Danielle Shay

She steps outside her front door — stillness.
A light wind touches her face.
She stares at the picture in front of her —
The sun— yellow with brightness,
The sky— a soft blue — cloudless,
The grass— a deep green,
The birds' friendly chirping just add to
The touch of peace instilled in her heart.

Her lips begin to hum a tune of zemiros
Known to her as a child,
but forgotten until now.
Surrounding her is peace — everywhere.
She strolls to a nearby lake not far from her home,
She sits,
She stares.

Stares at the green frogs splashing in the lake,
Stares at the little tadpoles following their mothers,
Stares at the lazy butterflies resting on the flowers,
Stares at peace.

Her hand reaches for the small leather book
inside her pocket.
The book is a Tehillim
She reads —
Peace.

Sometimes you don't realize how lucky you are until something that you take for granted is gone.

We had a problem with the hot water in our house. When we got it back I was so happy. I had this terrific feeling when the hot water came back. How lucky we are. Washing the dishes used to be such a boring thing to do but now that we got the hot water back I wanted to do it. What a good feeling!

Chaya Sarah W.

Imagine not having steam. During the freezing winter we would have to go to sleep with layers and layers of clothes to keep ourselves warm. With so many layers we would not even be comfortable. If we were to wake up in the middle of the night, we would be shivering. I feel like this because my mother doesn't give steam at night as my family has bad allergies.

In the morning if we wouldn't have steam, we would all wake up shivering. I know this because once when our steam broke we were so cold that we couldn't even get out of bed. *Baruch Hashem* for the money to afford steam.   *Blumie G.*

I'd like to take the time to mention,
A teenager's most cherished invention.

When you are bored at home
or feel alone,
Just pick up a telephone.

Dial a relative, neighbor or friend
And they'll pick up at the other end.

Have a short chat
Or a long conversation
To cope with a deep frustration.

I've come to the conclusion
That many people would be in seclusion.

Can you imagine how life would be
Without a telephone?

Sara Rivka K.

2-Minute Tips

✍ Quick Ways to Find Joy

Here are three antidotes to panic. When things go wrong, these ideas that were contributed by workshop participants can help you relieve the tension.

1. Smile Break.

Scientists have found that experiencing positive emotion, whether it's a giggle or a grin, can make us feel better. Dr. Annette Goodheart says, "We don't have to be happy to laugh. Indeed we become happy because we laugh."

(*Health Remedies and Techniques,* page 320)

2. A small success brings a larger success — Do one bite-size part of the overwhelming task that you have to face. If you have to clean your room for Pesach, choose one drawer and finish it. When you see that neat area you will feel like doing more.

3. Take a break from worrying and hold a child on your lap. Young children remind us that we are special just as we are. There is a beautiful innocence to their genuine affection. They respond to our attempts at conversation and song with sincere excitement. They can always help us feel better.

Now I Know!

- Life is a precious gift and there is always an opportunity for something good every day.

- In one minute you can change your attitude. That one minute can change your whole day.

- Three rungs to the ladder of happiness are:
  PLAN AHEAD
  BE PREPARED
  YOU CAN ALWAYS HELP

- When you aren't busy complaining, you'll be able to see how Hashem helps you.

Chapter 3

> Once a builder signed a contract obligating himself to build a structure for a certain fixed price. Upon completion of the building, the builder was paid the agreed-upon price, yet the builder wanted more. "You must pay me extra for the foundation!" argued the builder.
>
> The landlord, however, adamantly refused to pay." When I signed a contract for the building, the foundation was certainly included. Can you imagine a building without a foundation? Without a solid base the whole structure is worthless and would surely collapse."
>
> Only on a solid base of good Midos can we build ourselves up personally.

(Rav Elya Lopian quoted in *A Letter for the Ages*)

Being Responsible

*F*act: the way to succeed is to be responsible and to make sure to do the right thing.

When we are faced with problems, we tend to create excuses. When we botch things up, we feel that we haven't failed if we can give a believable reason. The first thing we might say is, "It's not my fault because he/she made me do it."

If you are on a diet and you eat a piece of cake you might say, "It's not my fault. I ate it because my mother bought it and left it in the refrigerator." It's embarrassing to make a resolution and then break it. We might feel frustrated with ourselves for having so little self-control. It's not fun to realize that dieting is harder than we thought it would be. Besides, cake tastes good. However, it's not our mother's fault we ate the cake. We are in charge of our actions.

Leah spoke in a defiant tone to the teacher and got into trouble. Leah might say, "When the teacher made me so angry, I answered back. I couldn't help it."

Rochel bought a watch that broke a week later. Rochel might say, "It's not my fault I bought it. The storekeeper made me take it."

Shuey and Yehudah are playing checkers. Yehudah keeps winning and Shuey feels frustrated. It's his game, he should win. When Shuey thinks Yehudah isn't looking, he jumps Yehudah's checker. "Hey, that's cheating," Yehudah says, "what did you do that for?" "Well, you keep on winning every game so I did it. You made me do it," Shuey says.

Sometimes people do something that makes us feel bad, or talk to us in a way that bothers us. We can't think straight when we are angry. We might think that it is their fault if we react and do something wrong. However, our behavior is our choice.

Leah might think the teacher wasn't being fair to her and Shuey might feel upset and embarrassed, but the teacher didn't "make" Leah answer rudely and Yehudah didn't "make" Shuey cheat.

When we blame someone else we feel a little better. We can pretend that everything is still fine and that this unpleasant thing didn't happen. Blaming others helps us pretend that we are perfect. We don't have to change; "they" do. We don't have to work on ourselves because even if we tried, it wouldn't make a difference.

If someone lends us their things we should make sure that they don't break and that they're returned in good condition. When we are left alone in the house we are responsible not to open the door to a stranger. We can't fall asleep when we are baby-sitting. If our parents give us a list of things to accomplish, we are responsible to take care of it.

Sometimes our actions or our character traits allow or

Chapter 3: Being Responsible ☐ 63

promote certain results. We might want to make believe that we aren't at fault, but it doesn't make the problem disappear. The truth is that many unpleasant events happen because we weren't careful, as the folk tale below demonstrates. The benefit in acknowledging our responsibility is that it gives us the power to remedy our situation.

> In the days of the horse-drawn wagons, a traveler arrived at a train station and hired a wagon. After giving the driver his destination, he cautioned him, "Please avoid this particular road. There is a deep ditch there."
>
> The driver started the horses. "Just sit back and relax, my friend," he said. "Don't worry. I have been driving these roads for thirty-five years."
>
> As they proceeded the passenger said, "I can see the way you are heading. Please don't go that way. The road there has that big pit."
>
> The driver smiled reassuringly. "No need to fear," he said. "I have been driving these roads for thirty-five years."
>
> Soon they turned off onto a path. The passenger hollered, "Hey! This is the path I told you to avoid. It has this great big ditch ahead."
>
> "Quit fretting," the driver said. "Haven't I told you? I have been driving these roads for thirty-five years."
>
> Before long, they reached the ditch and fell in, wagon, horse, and passenger. The driver crawled out from beneath the wreckage.
>
> "Funny thing, I swear," he said. "I have been driving these roads for thirty-five years, and every time I pass here, this is what always happens."
>
> (Generation to Generation)

How aptly this story describes our human tendencies! We go on the same path day after day, unwilling to admit that we have released control over our behavior; and — just like the driver in the story — we only realize when it's too late.

If you lost some money you might say, "It's not my fault I lost my dollar. My mother should have sewn up the hole in my pocket."

If you forgot your lunch you might say, "It's not my fault I forgot my lunch. My mother should have put it in my briefcase."

Everyone forgets at times and sometimes we might prefer to rely on someone else to remember those little things that are important like the hole in our pocket or our lunch. How do we handle our responsibilities? Do we sit back and wait for the familiar startled feeling to come over us? "Oops, my homework is missing!" "Oh, no! Where did my library card go?" Does it fix the situation if we rely on someone else?

Do we feel good about relying on others to take care of everything for us? At first glance it's more convenient to let others worry about every little thing for you. However, when you take care of yourself you are becoming mature. When grownups see that you are able to do ordinary things by yourself, they begin trusting you to take care of the things *you* want to do. When we change the way we act, a lot of things will come our way that we don't have now. Our parents won't nag us as much, our life will be more organized, people will listen to us, and we will accomplish much more.

It's obvious that people are much happier with you and you don't get into trouble when you are responsible. But being responsible gives you something even more important than that.

↞ Responsible People Feel Good Because They Know They Can Do Things Well.

A person is not trapped by what has happened to them in the past. We can change and grow. We can stop the habit of making excuses.

● We can decide to plan ahead and pack our briefcase at night.

● We can decide to stay calm and count to ten before we say something that will make the other person feel bad.

- We can decide to be on time.

- We can decide to take care of finishing a job without extra reminders.

Being responsible doesn't mean that you will never make a mistake again. We can't expect to be perfect. And that is OK. We don't have to be perfect. Grownups make mistakes sometimes too. We just have to know that when we make a mistake we can admit that we are responsible, and then move ahead and do better next time.

✎ What Does Being Responsible Mean?

If someone tells us, "You were responsible," we might think it means we are wrong and therefore we are bad or a failure.

That definition makes us feel weak and helpless. It leaves us stuck in a cycle of failure and doesn't let us get ahead. However, that's only half of what being responsible means.

Responsibility also means that we are old enough now to make some decisions on our own. People can trust us and depend on us. Although we have made a mistake, we also have the ability to do better next time.

To help us concentrate on preventing future problems by planning ahead and learning from what happens to us, Terrence Des Pres (author of *The Survivor,* a book about the Holocaust) divided the word responsibility into the two-word phrase — RESPONSE-ABILITY.

Terrence Des Pres explains the phrase "Response-ability" as follows: What is our **response** to a given situation? We should **respond** to the best of our **ability**. Realize that each of us has the **ability** to respond. There are things that we are able to do now to either correct the situation we are presently in or to learn from this situation for next time.

While feeling guilty and depressed gives us permission to blunder again, being response-able helps us to become better. We promise ourselves to change. We consider what will help us so that the blunder won't happen again. We don't waste our time grumbling, but instead we do what we can. If we make a sincere effort we will succeed. As the Talmud says, הַבָּא לְטַהֵר מְסַיְּיעִים אוֹתוֹ, one who tries to become better is guided by Hashem (*Shabbos* 104a).

Responsibility gives you tremendous energy. If you really feel that you must learn to be better, Hashem will help you. With sincere effort you will succeed.

This idea doesn't apply only to each individual. Terrence Des Pres documents the fact that nobody survived the Holocaust without help from others.

> *Response-ability is the ability to respond when you see someone in trouble. The people who helped (in the Holocaust) felt compassion for the suffering of others, and that compassion closed the distance between their own condition and that of another. And so they acted, bound in the oneness of humanity.*
>
> (*The Survivor,* Terrence Des Pres).

All Jews are one unit. Every Jew is responsible to help other Jews in every way he can. When we see that someone is in trouble, we shouldn't just shrug our shoulders and say, "What can I do?" We are responsible to help in some way. As *Rashi* comments, כָּל יִשְׂרָאֵל עֲרֵבִים זֶה לָזֶה (*Rashi, Vayikra* 26:37).

Rina compared this to a play. In a play each person has a part. You are responsible to do your part well even if it's just two lines. If you mess up your part of the play, the entire play will be a flop. In the same way, each of us has a part to do for *Am Yisrael,* that no one else can do for us.

✒ Interview

Through the thousands of years of exile, hardship, and wandering, Jews have demonstrated their faith in Hashem and their loyalty to the ideals of the Torah by caring for each other and helping each other. This tradition continues as Rina related in a recent interview.

Roiza: When has someone you know shown concern when they had an opportunity to help someone?

Rina: My cousins, while walking in midtown Manhattan, noticed a suspicious-looking person carrying a *streimel* box. They discussed what to do. One brother said, "Let's see what he has." The other brother agreed, "Yes, let's see if the fellow is willing to sell it, then I can buy it and return it to the owner."

The seller took out a truly well-made *streimel* of top-quality fur, that was probably worth $4,000. They negotiated with the thief. At first he asked for $150 but they bargained him down to $120.

Roiza: They had to overcome many barriers to help out here. Many people wouldn't want to talk to a thief at all, and they risked a sizeable sum of money. Who would know how difficult returning the *streimel* could be ? How did they return it?

Rina: They called a friend who works in advertising and he put an advertisement about the stolen *streimel* in the newspaper. His wife took the calls. There were about twenty calls. Finally one person called who described the *streimel* with all its identification marks exactly. The description of the box matched and the design on the band matched. The person they returned the *streimel* to, coincidentally, was a relative of my cousin who had bought it from the thief.

Roiza: Your cousin who bought the *streimel* originally from the thief must have been pleasantly surprised that he helped out someone he knew. How did he feel after reaching his goal?

Rina: He felt that the whole opportunity to help was a gift from Hashem. The *streimel* was stolen on Sunday and it never missed a Shabbos. This relative lives in Monsey and had come with his family to Williamsburg for Shabbos to visit someone who is ill. On Sunday they went to a restaurant. When they came out, they saw that their car window was broken and all their Shabbos clothes were stolen. The only item they got back was the *streimel*.

Everyone helped to return the *streimel* — the man who bought it, the friend who works in advertising, the newspaper that donated the ad space, and the woman who took the calls.

Roiza: Why do you think this incident is encouraging?

Rina: We can always use a success story to help us understand that it's important to feel responsible to do good when it arises. This story is an inspiring example of how Hashem cares for us and how Jews care about each other.

Exercise

Responsibility And Time

How did you find out that it is important to be punctual?

_____

_____

_____

_____

What are your feelings about being on time?

_____

_____

_____

_____

Actual Responses

Time. Ticking. Seconds. Minutes. Hours. Time.

The entire world lives on time. The businessmen constantly glance at the small little face on their left hand. Their world depends on time. Appointments, meetings, everything is contingent on time.

Passengers. They check the flight number, and the tickets again. Their plane is leaving promptly at 12:30 p.m. They glance at the small little face on their left hand.

Students. They check their books, school assignments, and tests. Their class is starting at 9 a.m. They constantly have to glance at the small little face on their left hand.

Every person has something different to accomplish but we all have one thing in common — the constant glancing at the face on our left hand.

Just in Time
Bryna Faigy Moskowitz

Try to imagine that one day
You didn't get up right away.
To get out of bed sometimes takes a day,
But today, do it just as fast as you may.

Your friend just called you
And told you, "Nu,
Outside in ten minutes you better be
Or else it's a detention for you and me."

You slip on your clothing and run out the door,
Just in time to get your second yelling for sure.
You explain that the alarm broke,
But to your teacher that's just a joke.

Then you find out that pens you forgot,
So you borrow a pen from someone

Just in time.
To fail the test you will not.

Because your money was lost on the way,
No lunch in school for you that day.
The day flew by very fast
And you are home now at last.

Now try to imagine
What would happen
If at ten you awake
And every limb does ache.

The room has no light,
You call someone with all your might.
You remember that your parents went away.
They will return in just one day.

Out of bed you do go,
Your walk is very slow.
Very slowly the day does pass.
You feel very lonely till they'll come home at last.

You check the time again and again.
If your aunt calls just then,
You'll thank Hashem for sending a savior
Even if they are doing only one small favor.

When the bell rings just in time
If it is your aunt or the dismissal bell
You will feel thankful and not think, well . . .

The clock read 8:30. I stared at it once more but none of the digits changed. I couldn't believe I had overslept again. It was the third time this week and it was only Wednesday! I hurriedly dressed myself, brushed my teeth and didn't eat breakfast. Breakfast is for the early birds who manage to awaken at the crack of dawn. At 8:46 I was ready. I ran, with my looseleaf in one hand and an apple in the other, as fast as my legs could carry me. I made it on time. Today was my lucky day.   *Yides B.*

"What! You are late again? What's the excuse this time?" Are these words ever addressed to you? If it's important to you to be on time, you make the effort. Last week as the morning sunlight shone through my window, I thought, "I wish I could go back to sleep." When I realized that it was Shabbos morning, I jumped out of bed. I hurried up and within minutes I was running down the block to *shul*. I came when they were not even up to *Baruch She'amar.*   *Nechama S.*

I was shopping with my sister for a family wedding that's coming up soon. We were in middle of trying on hundreds of dresses, but we made sure to stop in time to get to our piano lessons. If the piano teacher arrives and is ready, she shouldn't have to wait for twenty minutes.   *Mati H.*

I woke up bleary eyed and tired at 8:45. I got ready as fast as I could. I gulped down a spoonful of someone's leftover cereal and rushed out of the house. Uh oh! It was 8:58. I got to school at 9:03. I tried to slip in but I was marked late. The day went from bad to worse when I realized I hadn't done my French homework, and I was sent out of class. At the end of the day I concluded that my troubles started when I began my day on the wrong foot by waking up late.   *Shaindy G.*

At a friend's house I met Diana who didn't even know how to make a *berachah*. I explained a few things about Judaism to her and she was interested and willing to listen. On Shabbos morning I took her to *shul* and introduced my friends to her. After Shabbos I got her phone number. Once a week I found time to call her. Even when I had homework to do or chores in the house, I still called her punctually once a week. Many times I folded laundry as we spoke. She's very smart and was considering a public high school with a program for gifted children. Just today I found out that she has decided to go to a yeshivah.

I learned from this that if you commit yourself to something, you cannot back down even though you have other things happening in your life. If my friend and I hadn't kept in touch, she would be in public school now. *Danielle S.*

My heart beat wildly as I raced down 15th Avenue picking up speed. I ran with every ounce of strength I had. It was the first day of high school and I planned to be there for the first time in my life before the bell rang. In elementary school being late was an everyday occurrence. Although it wasn't all that pleasant, it never bothered me enough to do anything about it.

Last summer I was forced to stay in the hot humid city all summer because I wasn't accepted to camp. I had applied in June. I had time on my hands and I spent my summer thinking about the past and the future. On August 2, I decided that my future would look a lot different than my past.

I decided that I'd have a reputation as the most punctual student in the whole school instead of being known as "the girl who has a million notes. . ."

I climbed the stairs in my new school, beginning a new chapter in my life. I let out a tired but accomplished sigh feeling just great.

Since then I've always been punctual everywhere and believe me it's so worth it! *Gitty Malky B.*

I make myself really nervous by waiting for the last night before the test to study. I have to start cramming everything into my head at once. My stomach starts turning and my head starts spinning. By 11:45 I'm on my bed with all my notes and my book. With my eyes half closed, I continue studying. I finally close my books at 1:30. I dream all night about failing the test. At 5:30 my alarm clock rings bringing me out of my nightmare. My stomach starts turning again. By the time I have to get ready for school I'm too nervous to walk so my father drives me and wishes me good luck. I'm still looking at my notes when the bell rings and the teacher walks in. When the test begins I hold myself still and start using my memory. Good luck ! (After the ordeal is over, I promise myself that I'll start earlier next time.)   *Blumie G.*

2-Minute Tips

1. Buy yourself a brand new notebook for your lists and promises. Get some new pens or freshly sharpened pencils. Just having these essential items on hand will alert the "inner you" that something different is about to happen.

2. Pause for a moment at the door, and check if you have everything you need. Repeat instructions and addresses to be sure that you have heard them correctly. Finish one task before you start the next one.

3. Whenever possible, gather the supplies you need for your plans. For instance, if you want to bake on Thursday, you might check the recipes at the beginning of the week so you can pick up the necessary ingredients when you are out on other errands. It's a lot better than running to the store for margarine when your cake batter is in the mixer !

4. Rav Yisroel Salanter said that external order causes inner order. Take the time to keep your room neat and your desk cleared. Remember, by deliberately keeping things neat you'll be more receptive to important information.

Now I Know!

- I am in charge of my actions.
- Even if someone makes me angry, it is not his/her fault if I do something wrong.
- When I take care of myself I am becoming mature.
- Responsible people feel good because they know they can do things well.
- RESPONSE-ABILITY — What can I do to fix this situation?
  How can I make a plan so that this mistake won't happen again?
- Every Jew is responsible to help other Jews in every way he can.
- Time is valuable and using it wisely and being punctual demonstrates that I appreciate this fact.
- Punctuality shows that I respect other people's time.

Chapter 4

> *Faith and trust in Hashem are two pillars of fire. They light up the path to a pleasant life. Whoever follows these two pillars will never stumble as he walks in the land of life. His ankles will never be weak. Disappointment and tragedy can't come near the one who has faith and trust in Hashem. Illness and injury won't come on him.*

(*Sefer Toldos Menachem*, Rav Nachum of Horodna)

True or False?

In the last chapter we learned that the excuses we tell others make problems worse, not better. Grownups are disappointed; they don't trust us next time and our problems do not disappear.

A myth is something people believe that has no basis in actuality. People believe it because it's been said over and over. We all carry around myths about ourselves that hold us back and block out our good feelings like clouds block the sun.

Myths are excuses that we tell ourselves. We don't even realize the harm of this negative talk because it's hiding in the gray corners of our mind where we aren't aware of it. If you feel hopeless or weak occasionally and are wondering why, a myth about yourself might be the cause.

✒ Because . . .

The "because" message sneaks up whenever we want to avoid working on things that are "not so much fun." I can't do this because... One of these days I'd like to try . . . but it won't work because . . . We avoid change, growth and challenges.

Sometimes through a suggestion or through something we learn, a seed of hope begins to grow inside us. We think, "Maybe I could do this better." As we approach the experience however, our fear and doubt surfaces. Instead of realizing that everyone has doubts and that we should persist despite those feelings (and perhaps succeed), we give up. Let's see how the "because" message applies in your life.

Exercise

Write down ten things you want to have or do in your life. The list can include experiences, achievements, qualities, and activities. Don't choose items that depend on others: "I want a full-time maid, so I won't have to clean my room." Pick things that depend on you: "I want to go to sleep on time," for example:

1. _____

2. _____

3. _____

4. _____

5. _____

6. _____

7. _____

8. _____

9. _____

10. _____

Choose two items that you can make happen now. Why haven't they happened yet? What is your "because" message?

1. I can't because . . . _____

2. It won't work because . . . _____

3. It's too hard, because . . . _____

This critical voice in us is so familiar that we don't even think of challenging it. Now however you are about to find out four myths that can be safely ignored. In the next four chapters we will deal with overwhelming limitations, paralyzing fear, embarrassing mistakes, and the dread of sharing our ideas. Clap your hands and dance around the room! These rules need not scare you anymore. Just ask Hashem for help and go ahead.

How do these mistakes and myths happen? The *Mesillas Yesharim* compares this to darkness. The threatening darkness causes people to see things that aren't really there. A tree appears to be an ominous person or a wild animal. (Have you ever sat up in bed in the middle of the night and imagined something scary was in your room, but when you turned on the light there was nothing there?) In the same way, without the light of the Torah we can perceive obstacles and problems that aren't real.

The Chofetz Chaim, in *Give Us Life*, says that the light of Torah causes the darkness in our lives to fade away. He reminds us that we can't drive darkness away by attacking it with weapons, but if we light a single candle, the darkness will disappear by itself.

In the chapters that follow, you will learn how to light a candle. When you look at obstacles in the light of Torah, you will see that you can take the small steps toward growth that are necessary to overcome them.

✑ To Overcome Obstacles

The "because" message sneaks up whenever we want to avoid working on things that are "not so much fun." This is compared to darkness that causes us to see things that aren't really there. When we shine the "light" of a Torah thought on our fear it disappears.

1. Be aware of the myth. When you feel anxious, stop and think. What am I saying to myself? Is it one of the four myths?

2. What Torah thought will help me challenge this unpleasant feeling?

3. Now that you have the right Torah thought, hold on to it. Whenever you feel low again, tell yourself that Torah thought immediately.

4. Finally, in your imagination predict the best possible outcome.

In the next four chapters we will begin to tear down four of the crippling myths that impede our progress, and we will discover just how insubstantial they really were. Answer the following questions as instinctively as you can.

True or False

- When Tova was in the third grade, she tried to learn how to knit. The stitches fell off the needles and there were holes in her scarf. In order to fix it, Tova had to tear out all the rows, even the good ones. Now Tova says, "I can't knit!"

> *Is it true that Tova can't knit? If you have tried something in the past and failed, is it true that you can't do it successfully now?*
>
> ☐ True   ☐ False

● Sara has to give a five-minute demonstration in front of the class this week. She has never spoken in public before and she feels almost sick. Her stomach hurts, her palms are damp, and her heart is beating quickly. Sara tells herself, "Everyone else did the demonstration so easily. If I'm tense now, I probably won't do well."

> *Is it true that Sara is the only one who feels nervous?*
>
> ☐ True   ☐ False

● Penina has to rewrite her composition because it has five mistakes. Penina feels so upset. "Why is it so hard to do a perfect job? I'll never be good at writing if I make so many mistakes," Penina says.

> *Is it true that if Penina makes mistakes, she won't ever be able to do that thing well?*
>
> ☐ True   ☐ False

● Kaila keeps many of her opinions to herself. For example, she really feels bad when people make fun of others, but she doesn't tell anyone because she doesn't want to be different.

> *Is it true that Kaila has to hide her real self? If Kaila disagrees with the group, does it mean that there is something wrong with her?*
>
> ☐ True   ☐ False

Maybe you know people like Tova, Sara, Penina, and Kaila. Maybe you would like to tell them, "Don't worry, I've felt the same way sometimes, but go ahead and try and you'll succeed." And you're right. Now let's take a look at each of these questions separately.

Chapter 5

> "Papa was in a state of excitement that was contagious. Charles Lindbergh was about to make the first nonstop solo flight from New York to Paris. The year was 1927. We anxiously awaited every bit of news.
>
> "He made it!" Papa ran into the house waving the newspaper with the glaring headlines: "Lindbergh Lands in France."
>
> Papa sat down in his armchair, caught his breath and exclaimed, "This is a preview of Mashiach's times when Hashem will gather the Jews from all parts of the world and fly them over the oceans to Eretz Yisrael, on eagles' wings." Papa pointed to the picture of the plane, "Doesn't it resemble a flying bird?"
>
> I peered closely at the photograph. Then I looked at Papa with wonder and thought, "Would I ever fly into the sky?"

(All for The Boss, Ruchoma Shain)

How to Gently Push Your Limits

We are all born with the talent and tools to contribute in a unique way to our world. Have you ever watched a baby imitate an adult they admire? Perhaps you've seen your younger brother or sister "*davening*." They hold the *siddur* in front of them at the precise angle you do. They sway back and forth and move their lips with a solemn expression. Often their *siddur* is upside down and you can't hold back a giggle when you watch.

This process is more than a game. It's the first step of learning. Every young child practices, watches, and imitates in a completely joyful and stress-free manner again and again. This leads to **unlimited learning**.

What did you learn when you didn't have limits? By the time

you were 16 months old, you were probably walking quite well — a process that's so complicated it would take the rest of this book to explain everything your brain has to know before you can do it. You mastered walking despite many difficulties. You fell, you were bumped, you looked funny, and when you tried to run you stumbled over your own feet. Why did you try again and again?

The answer is, you had no concept of failure and you enjoyed the process. Every little success was exciting for you.

My 13-month-old daughter is wearing her first pair of shoes, thank G-d! She took her first steps three weeks ago. It began with that magic moment when she decided to let go of the table, sail off into the wide-open space, and take three courageous steps into my arms. To her delight, her four older siblings were all there to cheer for her and applaud her triumph. All that afternoon, her brothers and sisters practiced with her. One sibling stood a few feet away and the others cheered and clapped when my toddler took three tiny steps. After a while she was not only increasing her steps but as she walked, she applauded herself. In her young mind, walking and clapping go together.

I watched my little one walking, smiling, and clapping and asked myself, "What does it take for adults to feel that they are a success? How many 'steps' do we have to take? How much do we have to accomplish before we applaud ourselves inside? Have we set up our lives in a way that makes happiness difficult and discouragement almost inevitable?

Limits, barriers, boundaries. How many are real? How many are created in our minds? Do we know this barrier is blocking our path or have we decided to give up before coming close enough to see if it's there ? When doing math, we skip the difficult problems. When playing dodgeball, we let ourselves get hit when we're tired. We give up playing piano or learning other new skills after we notice we are making mistakes.

A woman who worked for a large municipal aquarium often saw an interesting phenomenon. Whenever the thick glass partitions in the main tank were pulled out to be cleaned, the fish would swim right up to the spot where the glass used to be, and just before crossing it they would turn back, warded off by a barrier that didn't really exist.

If you were watching these fish, would you feel like tapping on the tank and calling out, "Yoo hoo, fish, don't stop now, there is no barrier limiting you"?

There is so much that is lost when we give up before we have earnestly tried. Hundreds of dreams lie buried within each of us that never see the light of day. When I look out my window now, I can see colorful, cheerful tulip blossoms. It's so marvelous to see them and feel that spring has come. How precious they are. How happy they make me. I planted them last year in May. The package said they would bloom in July. Nothing happened in July or August. I waited and looked for almost a year. A gardening expert told me, "Don't give up, tulips have to go through the winter. They'll come." Now the tulips are here. In fuchsia, purple, bone, and yellow they say, "Don't give up, your efforts will bear fruit." Humans should be smarter than fish, but many times we are prevented from getting ahead by an obstacle that was once there in the past but is gone now for a long time. Sometimes after experiencing difficulty when attempting a new thing we never try again. We don't stay with the new craft long enough to master it. Often our relationships suffer because once someone has pushed us away we won't approach them again. In the worst case, our personality becomes defined by our past mistakes.

✌ The Past Is no More

We are told in no uncertain terms that no matter what we have done in the past, we should never view ourselves as inherent failures:

> A person should never see himself as intrinsically bad. The wrong he has done is something that passes, something that can be cleansed and fixed. As G-d said to Avraham, "You said to the guests (the angels who

came to visit after Avraham underwent Bris Milah), 'Let some water be brought and wash your feet.' I promise you that I will repay your children; they will be able to wash their souls."

The sin is only a covering, but the essence of the person is pure. When the sin is removed, he becomes a new person. (*Yalkut Meam Loez, Parshas Vayeira*)

How do you get started on a difficult task?

If in the past something was difficult, that doesn't mean that we will fail now if we try to do it again. We have all heard the words, "If at first you don't succeed, try, try again."

We remind ourselves that this is true whenever we need to motivate ourselves to try again. We push ourselves to try again when we have felt embarrassed. We push ourselves to say I'm sorry to our friend even though we feel that she should apologize first. We know that this is the only way to get beyond yesterday's distress.

A. Enthusiasm

If we really feel enthusiastic we can succeed despite past failure. Rina told us in a recent interview how she successfully accomplished something that had always been difficult for her.

Interview

Roiza: Many people have big goals, but they don't reach them because they have failed in the past. When were you determined to achieve a goal — no matter what?

Rina: In the past it has always been difficult to ask people for money. I have my own business yet I was ready to give it up because it's difficult to ask for a fair price or to insist on the customers paying their overdue bills.

Now I was in a spot. There was a really good cause and I wanted to help. A little town in Russia that I had visited needed a food mixer. How would I get it? I couldn't imagine where I'd find the money. Raising funds was no pleasant task for me. It's hard to ask for money when I feel I've earned it, so how was I going to ask people to give for a *Tzedakah*?

Roiza: How did you convince yourself that you should ask for money this time ?

Rina: I just couldn't say no. Velednik is a small town in Russia. Many Jews there are becoming *Shomer Shabbos* now. Food is very scarce and people literally cannot make Shabbos on their own. Every week there are four rooms filled with people who come to the communal kitchen for the Shabbos meal. Their gefilte fish looks like a black matzah ball — the kind you make on Pesach out of *Shemurah Matzah* flour. There's a spoonful of grated carrots next to it. Then they have soup, *kugel,* and a small piece of *challah*. There is a tremendous kitchen in Velednik where all the food is prepared. The kitchen needed a mixer. All the *challah* was prepared by hand and it was a very difficult task.

From where would the $400 come ? I couldn't say no to the Jews in this heroic town. They have been through so much and they have so much courage. You can't imagine how scarce food is. A potato is as large as an egg. The carrots are as large as my thumb. Nothing seems to grow well. In a short time however dozens of families were becoming *Shomer Shabbos*.

That last Shabbos before I left, I sang *zemiros* with the women. We sang *Oy Oy Oy Shabbos* over and over. I said, "Every Shabbos sing this *niggun* and I'll sing it along with you in America and it will be like I'm holding your hand here."

Roiza: How did you overcome your shyness and raise the money?

Rina: I mentioned it to everyone I met. I said to everyone, "Give something, it doesn't matter how much. Have a part in the *mitzvah*." One person gave $10 and one $7 and so on.

Roiza: So when you spoke with people you stressed what they were gaining. They were gaining a part in the *mitzvah*. You seem to have learned a lot about talking to people. How can other people discover when it's good to ask for something?

Rina: Before you ask, you have to be prepared. You have to really feel that you aren't doing it for personal reasons — to promote yourself, for honor, or to feel like a hero. When you make the request, think about the other person or cause and not about yourself.

As I was about to leave, I met someone in front of my house. She was worried about a serious problem. I said, "I have this wonderful *mitzvah,* take a part in it and Hashem will help you." She gave me whatever was in her pocket. It was only $7 but it's not important if it was a little or a lot. She gave it with her whole heart and I'm sure Hashem will help her.

Roiza: Did you manage to raise all of the money in time?

Rina: I still needed $200 which I advanced from my money. My husband collected it from the people who were flying with us to Russia.

Now I'm advancing that $200 towards something else they need in this town to advance *Yiddishkeit.*

Exercise

The teacher asked for volunteers. . .

When did you courageously offer to do a difficult task despite inner doubt ?

_____

_____

How did you feel afterward?

_____

_____

Actual Responses

The teacher asked for volunteers. A mother in the neighborhood had a newborn infant and needed help. Could anyone go to help for two hours after school? I hesitated. I felt shy to go to a stranger's home. Would I be able to handle this? Who could know what I was getting into? My friend motioned that we should go together. When I went into the tiny apartment I was shocked by the mess, the broken furniture, and the crowded conditions. I had never seen anything like it.

My steps were light as I walked home two hours later. I felt proud and grateful. The familiar stone steps in front of my house looked like marble. I opened the door and was overcome by the warm and pleasant ambiance. My ordinary dining room was a ballroom and my standard kitchen better than the ones in the magazines.

My bedroom felt like a warm and comforting cocoon after my friend and I had cleaned the woman's house for two hours. How wonderful it felt to be me.

I had hesitated to volunteer to help. I'm glad I did.

When our main teacher was organizing the annual student *Melaveh Malkah* I was chosen to take care of the entertainment. I was feeling a little uneasy at first; so many things could go wrong. It was a big responsibility because I had to handle a dance, a skit, and a choir. In the past when I had only been a helper I noticed that things can go wrong at the last minute.

When I discovered it was just too much pressure, I asked my fellow classmates to help me out. They were so nice to work with. We were a great team.   *Devorah R.*

During color war in school, I was asked to write a twenty-minute speech to be delivered by two other girls and me. My head started to ache with worry. When I have to write something it usually comes out good in the end, but no one realizes how hard I try because of the many early drafts that I toss into the garbage. This time it would have to be really good. My whole team was counting on me. What would I say?

I asked two other girls if they would join me in giving the speech. They offered not only to perform with me but also to help me write it. I thought it would be a long tedious job, but it turned out to be fun because I had my two friends to help.

Devorah S.

At the nursing home they really needed visitors. At first I wondered whether or not to go. Would I be a help or would I just make things worse? I worried that I would feel so awkward and I wouldn't know what to say. I went anyway. The nursing home is over a mile away from my house. I walked alone every Shabbos. Now close to 10 girls come with me each Shabbos.   *Malky T.*

Last year when I was in the eighth grade I was asked to perform a solo dance at the concert. The concert hall seats over 1500 people, and just thinking about the number of people that were to be there made my stomach tie up in knots! I knew this job was too big for an eighth grader to do alone. I vaguely knew a girl in the twelfth grade who was a great dancer. I hesitated to go to her. Why would a twelfth grader want to help an elementary school girl?

Finally I got up the courage and explained my situation to her. To my surprise she readily agreed to help me. Almost every night a month before the dance, she would come over to my house. She choreographed the dance, found the music, and helped me through it all. She also gave me encouragement and guidance. The dance was a success.

Leah T.

2-Minute Tips
To Help You Push Your Limits

1. **Are you open to change?**

   In order to fill a drawer with the supplies you need, you have to first clear the drawer of clutter. What bad habits are cluttering your life and preventing achievement?

2. **Are you willing to give yourself time to change?**

   Have you ever been at a lecture and resolved to change a certain trait **from now on?** How quickly did you give up? In *Shaarei Teshuvah,* Rabbeinu Yonah says that if you want to improve you should expect to need consistent reminders for at least a month.

3. **Are you willing to ask experts how to do things better?**

   When one moves into a new house there is the opportunity to make a fresh start. Before I moved I visited several expert "Balabustas." I learned many important tips this way — such as, the type of flooring that looks clean longest and that clothes closets need to be deep while the pantry and book shelves can be shallow.

4. **Are you determined to enjoy your progress although you only succeeded partially?**

   Enjoy your progress. Was your attempt at least partially successful? Make a list of the things that were accomplished and give yourself 30 seconds to enjoy each one.

Now I Know!

- **Are waves of doubts upsetting your plans?**
  Is the obstacle *real* or have you given up too quickly?
  Hashem has promised that leaving the past behind will be easier than we expect if we make the effort.

- **Do you feel bored or irritated?**
  Avoiding obstacles feels comfortable for a while; however, it also makes us feel bored and empty. We know inside that we are on earth for something more and that causes a restless feeling.

- **Whenever the thick glass partitions are pulled out, do you swim toward a higher goal?**
  Like Rina, we can go beyond our limitations when we focus on the results, know there is a real need, and ask Hashem for the courage to push on.

Chapter 6

" *Instead of being anxious about every little detail of our lives we should concentrate on fearing Hashem. If we do this, Hashem will take care of all our other fears.*

In the Midrash there is a parable about this: Two people had fields. One lived in Teveria and had a field in Tzipori. The other from Tzipori had a field in Teveria. They both struggled to manage their properties from afar. Finally they struck a deal with each other, "I'll care for your field and you care for mine." So too, Fear of Hashem is on earth and everything else is from Heaven, as it says, הַכּל בִּידֵי שָׁמַיִם חוּץ מִיִּרְאַת שָׁמַיִם, *all is in the Hands of Heaven except for Fear of Hashem. Hashem says to us, "You take care of serving Me and I'll take care of you."* "

(Pele Yo'aitz, Daagah)

Freedom From Fear

At the class we were discussing the tension surrounding family parties. Etty said, "I prepare a week in advance." Tammy said "I'm up the night before worrying." Shira said, "I don't worry; I just take care of everything on the day of the party." Rivka said, "I have never made a party. I can't take the stress."

Freedom to Explore New Things

Have you ever wondered in frustration, "What stops me from trying new things? Why do I say, 'I just can't; I'll fall on my face? Why do I decide I can get by without ever doing that particular thing? Why do I feel that since I can't stretch, my goals will just have to shrink?' "

Our anxiety is aggravated when we tell ourselves that we are the only ones who feel this way. We think that everyone else does new things perfectly well as soon as they decide to try. Since our friends never admit their doubts and seem so calm on the outside, we deduce that we are the only ones who ever hesitate and worry.

וַיָּבֹאוּ בְנֵי יִשְׂרָאֵל בְּתוֹךְ הַיָּם בַּיַּבָּשָׁה וְהַמַּיִם לָהֶם חוֹמָה מִימִינָם וּמִשְּׂמֹאלָם, *the Children of Israel came within the sea on dry land, and the water was a wall for them, on their right and on their left* (Shemos 14:22).

Rabbi Meir says, "When the Jewish nation stood by the *Yam Suf,* they competed with each other, and each one said, 'I will go into the sea first.' " Rabbi Yehudah says, "However when they actually faced the waters of the sea, each one said, 'No, I can't go first.' Then Nachshon the son of Aminadav jumped forward into the sea" (*Sotah* 36b, 37a).

We learn that when we are about to act we become filled with doubt and we hesitate. Therefore the Jews hesitated and regretted their initial resolution until Nachshon came and jumped into the sea (*Hagaon Rabbi Yehoshua of Kutna*).

Fear isn't wrong or right, bad or good. When you are afraid, remember you aren't alone. Everyone feels afraid sometimes; it's normal. Understanding and accepting this makes it possible to push ahead despite your fear. Two positive emotions that are partners with fear are love and trust. When we love someone, we are afraid he/she might get hurt. When we want to trust a friend, we are afraid he/she might become distant from us in the future. Nobody can "make" you feel a different way. Sometimes we can't stop worrying about the possibility of anything going wrong.

How do you feel about your fears? We may feel embarrassed or self-conscious about telling anyone how we feel. (Will other people think I'm not mature?) We may censor our thoughts because we worry about creating a self-fulfilling prophecy. (If I think about it, it might happen.) We may feel guilty thinking bad thoughts. (Shouldn't I trust her? She's my friend.)

You are stronger than your fear. Listen to the little voice in you that says, "You can do it!" That voice is right.

I know my baby can walk and I coax him to try. G-d, too, knows that we can do great things and tries to coax us to go for it. G-d tells us every day, "You are My children. You are a kingdom of priests and a holy nation."

✐ How Can We Overcome Our Fear?

A. Know that you are not the only one.

When we compare ourselves to others, we usually don't look at those who are struggling but rather at those who have a lot of experience. We hesitate on the side of the skating rink and watch the girl in the middle doing "figure eights." If we look to the side however, we would notice quite a few other people who are also filled with doubt.

When you observe from the outside, everything looks so easy and smooth. This poem describes the struggle that goes on beneath the surface to ensure success.

> *I walk along the water*
> *and I gaze out to the sea.*
> *I see two boats called friend-ships*
> *gliding on so gracefully.*
>
> *They seem a natural perfect pair*
> *to my unknowing eyes,*
> *But I know not of their struggles*
> *nor their pain and compromise.*
>
> *And emotions that they share,*
> *Those of love and hope and pain,*
> *Will help polish their interior*
> *And help them both to gain.*

Oh, I walk along the water
and I look out to the sea.
I see two boats called friend-ships
gliding on so gracefully.

And they're using everything they have
to make this success last.

Malky Zelcer

Everyone was once a beginner. Everyone has to struggle to learn a new skill, make a new friend, acquire wisdom, and do things easily. Many people who are a success to-day failed dozens of times when they began. The difference is they kept at it until they succeeded and you can succeed too.

B. Ask Hashem to help.

The eagle decides to go on a long journey. The eagle does not want to abandon its young birds. The babies must come along, but they are sleeping in the nest.

The eagle could immediately wake them. "Wake up! Climb up on my back. We are going on a long trip. Hurry!"

But you don't waken baby eagles abruptly. That could harm them. So how does she do it? She hovers over the nest. She flutters back and forth and touches the little ones with the edge of her wings. She flies away and comes back again and again. Slowly and gently they awake.

The Vilna Gaon explains: When Hashem came to take us out from Egypt, He had to wake us up. Through the plagues that Hashem brought upon Egypt, we were aroused from our numbness and dejection. There were two aspects to each plague: The Egyptians were punished and the Jews were saved. After the tenth plague we were "fully awake" and could be taken out of Egypt.

Why does the eagle have to awaken the young birds? Isn't the eagle in charge? The babies are only passive riders. If I go for a long bus ride, it is all right if I fall asleep. After all, it's the bus driver who has to be awake and alert.

The eagle's wing is not a bus or car, however. It's like being *outside* an airplane! If the eagle falls asleep, the babies could fall off. Those baby eagles have to hold on with all their strength.

Every milestone and every level that we ever reach is because Hashem Himself has lifted us there.

What does Hashem want of us? That we should not sleep away our lives. We should use every opportunity to the fullest extent. Hashem tells us to be wide awake and to hold on with all our strength and He will take us higher and higher. *Rav Shlomo Brevda*

C. Use the power of determination and imagination.

One of the main components of man is his sense of purpose and will. The energy that determination generates can overcome our limitations. Spend a few minutes deciding that you truly want to do something. Really feel a sense of resolution. If a person wants to do Hashem's will, that yearning will bring him to action. The feeling of determination is the crucial beginning.

The Talmud describes a peddler who trudged from town to town and called out, "Who wants to buy the potion of life?" When crowds gathered he took out the Book of *Tehillim* and read, "Who is the man who wants to live? . . . He should guard his tongue from speaking bad."

The Rav of Ostrow explained that there are two steps to the magic potion of life that the peddler sold. The first step is to YEARN to serve Hashem and the second step is to Guard Your Speech. As the "Yehudi Hakadosh" said, "Even if you have only the yearning to reach the level of wanting to serve Hashem, you are already considered God's servant."

At a recent workshop, I asked, "Have you ever found in some unexpected way that your yearning led to an opportunity to act?"

Ayala said, "When I lived out of town my close friend demonstrated tremendous respect and loyalty to her parents. My parents lived miles away then, but I thought about it and kind of wished, 'I hope someday I can do the *mitzvah* of honoring my parents on a daily basis.' Eventually we moved back to New York and now, these past three years, my mother-in-law lives with us."

What is the desired outcome? Imagine yourself doing this new thing with vitality and energy. What feeling would you have if you knew how to do this well? Picture yourself at a time in your life when you succeeded and create images of the present, feeling just that way.

D. Come out of hiding, jump in and act.

If you ever performed in a play, you know that nervous feeling when the curtain opens. The audience is so big. This is your first time. You were hiding behind the curtain — now you feel exposed. What if you make a mistake? You wish the curtain would close again. But there isn't even time to hesitate. You step forward, say your lines as you rehearsed them and everything is fine.

The problem with the fear of trying new things is that the only way to overcome it is through practice and experience. You have to act. The first time is difficult, it might even feel like you are closing your eyes and jumping into the sea. However, after you face your fear and succeed, it gets easier and easier. One day you will look back and wonder why you were ever afraid of this particular thing in the first place.

2-Minute Tips
Coping with Nervousness on Crucial Days

1. **Be Prepared** — When you prepare all the minor things *you* can control, you will feel less flustered. Make sure you have all your supplies. If you need an electrical appliance, make sure it works.

2. **Eat Carefully** — When you are nervous it's especially important to eat nutritious and balanced meals. One person I know ate four chocolate bars before an interview to apply for a seminary overseas. By the time it was her turn to be interviewed, she had a bad headache and could not perform well.

3. **Be on Time or a Bit Early** — Give yourself a few minutes to gather your resources before you start. Look over your notes, get your supplies ready, double-check the room. When you arrive late and run in breathlessly, you feel even more nervous.

4. **Get Support** — If you know someone composed and reassuring, speak to them. Moods are catchy. Hopefully the level-headed person's serenity will calm and encourage you.

Now I Know!

- I am not alone when I feel afraid. Everyone feels anxious sometimes. Understanding this makes it possible to push ahead despite fear.

- When one's will is strong, he can face his fear. The feeling of determination is the crucial beginning.

- One day I will look back and wonder why I was ever afraid of this particular thing in the first place.

Chapter 7

> Why do we eat farfel (a side dish of toasted egg barley) as part of the Shabbos eve (Friday night) dinner menu?
>
> It is said that this tradition began with the Baal Shem Tov, who exploited a play on words for a symbolic teaching.
>
> The word "farfallen" in Yiddish means "bygone" or "over and done with." The Baal Shem Tov taught that when one realizes the mistakes or wrongdoings that one has committed, sincerely regrets them, and makes a sincere resolution never to repeat the same act again, that is the essence and totality of repentance.
>
> Essential to the growth process is a release from the albatross of the past. Shabbos is the time for teshuvah (returning) to the correct path in life. Mother reminded us of this every Friday night as she served the farfel tzimmis. "Remember, whatever was until today is farfallen."
>
> Lebedig, kinderlach, lebedig.

(Generation to Generation, Rabbi Twerski, pages 47-48)

Beginning Anew — Learning From Our Mistakes

✍ True or False

1. A white dress, white couch, and white rug must never get dirty.
2. You can always take charge of your life. The answer is there. You just have to find it.
3. Everyone else is without blemish. You are the only one with a flaw.
4. If you made a mistake, you are a mistake.

The answer to every statement above is obviously false. Yet as one workshop participant so aptly commented, "Although we know these messages aren't true, we feel like they are." Do you constantly aim for everything around you to be perfect? Do you wonder why things never measure up to your expectations?

Dr. Steven J. Hendlin, clinical psychologist and author, says that "perfection is a fantasy." If something is flawless, it is probably not authentic. Diamonds teach us this lesson. Every real diamond has a flaw; only the imitations are perfect. Diamonds are a natural product and they always will have tiny particles of carbon in them. When you look at a diamond you may notice the flaw as dark spots. However, imitation diamonds have no carbon; they are clear glass all the way through, so they are "perfect."

Everyone wants and needs to feel safe, but we have to balance that against living our lives fully. There is a deep happiness that comes from new experiences. Competency doesn't happen all at once. The important concept to attain is that you can enjoy every level of the "step-by-step" learning process.

Have you heard people say, "Do it right the first time"?

That's an unrealistic goal. It only causes us to say, "I really don't feel much like doing anything new."

The pressure to be perfect tempts us to find someone else who we are sure can do it right.

Do you write your own compositions? Do you draw your own posters? Is your homework your own work?

When I was in second grade the teacher asked me to make a poster for the *Parshah* of the week. When I asked my mother to do it, she said," You draw nicely and I'm sure you can do it." I drew a picture of a tent that looked like a triangle. It had a lot of flowers around it. Then I wrote Avraham *Avinu* on top. My mother said, "It's beautiful!" When I got to school someone said, "Your *Alephs* are backwards — they look like an X." The next week someone brought in a professional poster. It looked like a work of art. However it was clear that my classmate's mother had made it.

Yes, it was painful to discover that my poster had its faults. I took that pain and channeled that energy to learn how to draw better. I practiced for hours and copied letters out of books. In the fifth grade when I made a poster everyone said, "Your lettering is so pretty, who made it for you?" I said, "I made it myself." That was a good feeling.

Do you feel good about doing your best or do you let someone else do it for you because it has to be perfect?

When my friend asked her two-year-old why he wasn't picking up the toys in the playroom he said, "Sima is doing it." "Well, why don't you clean too?" the mother asked. "Sima does it better, she knows exactly where everything goes" was the reply.

Unfortunately many people are afraid to make mistakes. They look for the easy way out instead. While that may be OK when they are two years old, if they continue that way throughout life their "helpers" will actually make them helpless. Their initial satisfaction and easy success will sour as they realize that the easy way has crippled them. When someone does it for you, you become dependent, hesitant, and childlike.

Don't deny yourself the pleasure of discovery. When you give yourself the freedom to be less than perfect, you are giving yourself the freedom to learn and grow. Each day you will grow more confident. Confidence only comes from action.

It's hard for us to learn from our mistakes because we feel bad about them. We think that someone else wouldn't have been as foolish as us. Someone with more experience could do it right the first time.

When you realize you've done something wrong, you might run into your room and bury your head in your pillow. You feel that you don't want to look at anyone or talk to anyone. You hear voices in your head — voices that say, "You are never good enough, you should be ashamed, you are a failure."

✒ Failure Is Temporary

The first thing to keep in mind is that failure is generally temporary. How many disappointments have you already forgotten? When you keep the proper perspective and realize that this too will fade from memory, just like the others, it is easier to get back on your feet. Depend on the hope and belief that next time things *will* go smoothly and your pain will be more limited. If you think you *will* succeed in the future, you will probably be right.

When you remain hopeful, you will understand mentally that with time the mistake will shrink, even though it feels unpleasant right now. You will be able to look back on this time and learn from it because it will no longer seem so crushing.

❧ Mistakes Are an Opportunity for Growth

If you can grasp the fact that making mistakes and correcting them is part of life, you will be able to forgive yourself. You will know that you can learn from your errors and you can do better next time. Instead of thinking, "I'll *never* do it right," you will look forward to your next attempt. You will think, "I don't have to be afraid of this. It is an opportunity and a challenge to find new skills and new strengths."

Eventually you will understand that everyone is less than perfect. People are not expected to be perfect, but they are expected to learn from their mistakes. If you can learn and improve your attitude, success and joy are waiting for you.

As a professional writer I have to deal with the indignity of submitting my writing to an editor. Despite my training, knowledge, and practice and although I had worked hard to perfect my manuscript on my own, the average page of writing has twelve to fifteen corrections. Often a phrase I treasured or even an entire paragraph I labored over is crossed out by the editor's red pen.

It took me a while to adjust to this process, because I have a strong perfectionist streak in me. For example, I've never learned how to knit because I know that when you make a mistake you have to rip out your work. I've also given up sewing to avoid opening up seams and starting over.

The turning point in my attitude toward writing happened ironically because of a mistake. When I printed out my manuscript, an excerpt that was two paragraphs long appeared on one page while the name of the expert I had quoted was on the top of the following page. My editor assumed that the entire page was written by me so she corrected the excerpt extensively. Phrases were deleted, commas were inserted, and words were changed. The excerpt was from a book that has been reprinted nine times and it was written by the editor of the publishing company!

When I saw this I laughed out loud. Now I no longer take my writing mistakes personally. I know that no writer can produce perfect copy, but one can do an excellent job. One can do work that is good enough to be enjoyed by many people. I've reminded myself of this incident over and over again when I feel like a failure. Mistakes are not only part of the writing process, they are a part of life.

Interview

Roiza: When did someone depend on you to take care of things?

Raizy: I came home one Friday afternoon to find my mother in a messy kitchen. The house smelled delicious. My mother smiled and said, "Raizy, you came home just in time. I'm leaving to buy a few items. Can you please clean up the kitchen?" As my mother ran out I heard her say, "Please turn off the oven downstairs in an hour."

Roiza: Did you get to work right away or did you just play around?

Raizy: I quickly ate lunch and set to work. I washed and dried the dishes. I had the kitchen shining in 20 minutes.

Roiza: That's great. Things were going really smoothly. I guess you thought you were doing a good job.

Raizy: When everything was finished, I thought I deserved a rest. I plopped down on the couch to read my book. I became drowsy and I must have drifted off to sleep.

Roiza: What happened when you woke up?

Raizy: I saw my mother standing there. "Raizy, you burned the cakes!" she cried out. I jumped up and ran down. I realized I had burnt a chocolate cake and a cinnamon cake. I felt terrible.

Roiza: You must have been disappointed. You didn't want to forget to do something important like turning off the oven. It happened by mistake, but the results were disastrous. What did you learn from this mistake?

Raizy: I learned a great deal. Now I don't rely on my memory alone. When my mother leaves me at home and tells me to turn off the gas, I post a note on the freezer. Sometimes I set the oven timer too. I want to be known as someone you can trust.

✏ What Are Your Skills?

When you feel bad about a mistake, you may find yourself saying, "Nothing ever goes right."

Remembering some of the things you've learned to do well in the past can help you feel better. There are talents you were born with such as the ability to sing well or dance well. There are skills you learned at home such as how to be organized or how to cheer people up. Finally, in school you have learned specific skills like understanding Torah commentaries, writing the perfect paragraph, or multiplication.

Your growth is amazing. Look at a pair of your first shoes. Don't you feel huge and different from those days? Did you save your first-grade notebook? Do you remember how you learned the sound of each letter by finding pictures of objects that began with that letter? Try to trace with your finger those big letters that took up two lines each. Doesn't it make you smile?

Every time you have a disappointment, go back and say, "Look how far I've come." Get ready to learn new skills every day. Your hard work will pay off!

2-Minute Tips
Preventing Mistakes

1. Concentrate

It is difficult to do many things at once. What task needs your immediate attention? Complete one item at a time.

2. Relax

If you are very tired, it's better to take a short break than to make mistakes and have to do things over.

3. Clear the Clutter

An uncluttered room makes for an uncluttered mind. An uncluttered briefcase will save you from losing or misplacing important things just when you really need them.

Now I Know!

- "Perfection is a fantasy." If something is flawless, it is probably not authentic. Every real diamond has a flaw.

- Mistakes are a part of the process (and pleasure) of learning.

- The attitude that next time things will go more smoothly is a sturdy base for getting beyond mistakes.

- When you feel bad about a mistake remember that there are many things you do well.

Chapter 8

Words Affect Our Lives

Even in the most seemingly meaningless chatter, the words that pass between people work powerful changes on them and within them. What a person says, what he hears, and what others say about him can surely change the course of his life.

(Chofetz Chaim/A Lesson A Day — Overview)

Say What You Believe

*I*t's hard to decide when to speak up and when to keep quiet. If you really believe that something is important, you should share your opinion. However, you might hesitate because you don't want your friends to criticize you. If you tell people how you really feel and they look at you strangely, you can feel stupid.

Sometimes when you know people are doing the wrong thing, you are afraid to talk about it. You don't want to sound like a goody-goody. You don't want to be labeled the "tzadekes."

Don't be afraid to stick to your values and express them. You may think that "everyone" is doing something. Yet "everyone" may be just one person who is the leader or most outspoken person and the rest are a lot of followers who are simply afraid to speak up.

Standing by your convictions shows you are mature. When you were young, you didn't have many ideas of your own. You worried about toys and dolls and how your barrettes looked. As your intellect develops, you begin to have more serious feelings and opinions. You notice you have deeper feelings about everything. You realize that life isn't that simple and you think more about fear, guilt, values, and what people are really like. When you were young, life seemed to be one way — perfect; now you notice things you've missed before and realize that life is much more complicated.

If you withhold and suppress these spiritual and emotional thoughts, you start to feel sad without knowing why. It seems easier to just ignore any thoughts that might make you feel different. However, you are putting limitations on yourself and your world. When you pretend, you fall out of touch with who you are.

My grandmother was always healthy and vibrant. Suddenly, when I was 14, she had a stroke. A few days later she was in a coma. I felt so alone, standing and writing her name on the board. Every day for three months I went to each class in the high school and wrote my grandmother's name, Chava bas Roiza, on the blackboard. I would announce, "Please pray for this person. It's very important." Yet I was often too shy to say, "This name belongs to my grandmother."

I learned so many concepts when my grandmother was *niftar*. That's when I grew up. That was when I realized that there will be times when all of us will know that "it's too late." It's too late to *daven* for the person; too late to send a letter; too late to visit; too late to learn from that precious person; too late... This time goodbye was forever.

I felt deeply, for the first time, that we must be on earth for something more. I had heard my teachers talk about all these lofty ideals before, but I had not been listening with my entire being. My life had been pretty smooth and my worries centered around everyday routine things. Now I was looking for ways to grow and develop inside. My grandmother was *niftar* in June. That summer, I found the Hirsch Siddur in the camp library. I had never realized before how beautiful our prayers are. I had probably understood only 30 percent of what I had been saying. I carried the *siddur* with me and tried to learn whenever we had a break in activities.

There were so many thoughts and feelings in me that I thought I would burst. I didn't understand where all these feelings were from or what to do about them. It was a very intense time in my life. Looking back, I think that praying was the best thing I could have done. It is always wise to talk to Hashem. He is always listening and He understands us best.

✌ Thinking About Your Feelings

Before you are ready to share your deeply felt ideas, you may want to think about them to yourself.

1. What are five things you feel strongly about?

2. Are you sure of your opinions?

3. How did you get your new idea? Was it from something that happened to you? From your family? From a teacher? From a book? From a friend?

4. Where does your opinion apply? Can you find specific examples where this fact in your mind proves true?

5. Do you act on your ideals in your own life?

Rav Yehudah Hanasi, or Rebbe, taught an important technique when communicating our feelings — always speak softly and kindly.

Rebbe invited his students to a festive meal and served them a delicacy — tongue. Some of the tongue was well cooked and soft while some was undercooked and hard.

When the meal was over, the platters bearing the soft tongue were empty while those with the hard tongue were still full.

Pointing to the full platters, Rav Yehudah said, "All of you chose the soft tongue and left the hard tongue untouched. This should be a lesson to you in life. You should always use a soft tongue, find the softest and kindest way to express your feelings. Put aside a harsh tongue, words said in a loud angry way."

Last year my sister Manya delivered a lecture on *Pirkei Avos*. She mentioned many things that she learned as a child from our parents and grandmother. I loved listening to her speak because she remembers things about my older relatives that I didn't know or have forgotten. She mentioned how when she was growing up she couldn't do things that were improper just to dance along with the crowd, because she was "a Perlman." Although it was hard at times to have to stand her own ground when she was growing up, as an adult she is proud of those same convictions. The seeds were planted when we were young and now we can see the flowers.

If you do take the chance and tell others what's right, the results could be great. People might compliment you because they were feeling the same way but they also kept it secret. Sometimes through sharing your convictions you can make a friend.

Sincerely saying what I believe has brought some dramatic changes in my life on many different occasions. My casual friendships reached a deeper level when I was honest. When I shared my ideas with others it led to a more meaningful relationship.

When I was a junior in high school, I finally had the chance to speak about my deep feelings when my grandmother was *niftar*. I spoke about the importance of praying sincerely for others. I concluded with this thought: "When I was in ninth grade, my grandmother fell into a coma. Until that time, whenever I had prayed for the sick people on the *Tehillim* list, I had thought of the list as a bunch of names. But when I wrote my grandmother's name on the list, it wasn't just a name. I wrote it with tears in my eyes, hoping that everyone would remember to pray for her. She was *my* grandmother. Please remember that every name on the list is someone's father, mother, grandmother, grandfather, son, or daughter."

When I came down from the podium, I was surrounded by my classmates. I remember one friend whose look was piercing. "When my father was sick, I also asked people to pray for him," she said to me. "When he recovered, I felt like I wanted to hug every person in the class. Roiza, thank you for telling everyone, because that is exactly the way it is."

From that time on this friend and I began spending more time together. We found that we not only shared the same ideals but that we both liked music and writing. We still call each other every year before Rosh Hashanah.

✎ Interview

Roiza: Did you ever feel that you really needed to share your feelings with others instead of suffering alone?

Shoshana: When I was only eight years old, I went through a nightmare. My younger sister Chavie was sick with cancer. I was only able to get through it with the help of my best friend.

Roiza: That must be one of the hardest things to go through in life. What were your feelings at the time?

Shoshana: I didn't know much about what was going on then but I knew it was bad. I was afraid she was going to die.

Roiza: When there is a family crisis, everything can seem to be turned upside down. In what ways were things different in your life?

Shoshana: I wasn't getting any attention, and I never saw my mother. I once visited my sister in the hospital, and she looked horrible. Really, deep down, I knew what was going on, but I didn't want to face it.

Roiza: Sometimes it can be hard to share feelings. Were

you able to talk openly? How did your friend help you overcome your doubts and uncertainty?

Shoshana: My best friend Miriam K. helped me through it a lot. When I didn't say anything about it, she didn't either. However as time went on when I wanted to talk about it, she listened. When I finished talking, she comforted me.

Roiza: Did your friendship become stronger because you were able to communicate openly?

Shoshana: Our talks during that year are probably the reason we are best friends. I will never forget what she did, especially since she was so young and inexperienced with such situations. I think it was a gift from Heaven that Hashem made her able to understand it all. She is the smartest and nicest person I have ever known, and I know my sister will watch over her forever.   *Shoshana S.*

2-Minute Tips

1. **Talk About Important Things for Five Minutes Every Day** — It takes courage to talk meaningfully. This courage will make your life more fulfilling.

2. **Accept Your Feelings** — There are times that everyone is angry, nervous, sad, disappointed, or discouraged. Don't feel embarrassed. When you recognize your feelings it's easier to find options for dealing with them.

3. **Describe What You Need Clearly** — Don't expect people to be prophets. Even if someone can see that something is wrong, if you refuse to talk about it, it's difficult for the person to know what you need or how to help.

Now I Know!

Congratulations! You've just found out the truth about four myths that hold people back from accomplishment. Remember these strengthening Torah thoughts throughout the week when you need them. Let us review the truth once again.

1. If we really feel enthusiastic we can succeed despite past failure. Every day we can learn new skills and successfully accomplish something that was difficult for us previously.

2. Fear isn't wrong or right, bad or good. When you think you are afraid, you aren't alone. Everyone feels afraid sometimes. However, listen to the little voice in you that says,"You can do it!" That voice is right.

3. When you give yourself the freedom to be less than perfect, you are giving yourself the freedom to learn and grow. Each day you will grow more confident. Confidence only comes from action.

4. After you have thought about your deeply felt ideas, consider sharing them with others. It's one way to build close friendships.

Every Time

- Every time you *daven* and say each word carefully, you are a success.
- Every time you forgive a sister or brother and don't hit back, you are a success.
- Every time you help out before you were asked, you are a success.
- Every time you listen the first time, you are a success.
- Every time you smile first, you are a success.
- Every time you say hello to a less popular girl, you are a success.
- Every time you remember to remove your plate and cup before you leave the table, you are a success.
- Every time you stop at the door and say have a nice day, you are a success.
- Every time you visit your younger brother in kindergarten, you are a success.
- Every time you say a *berachah* loud and clear, you are a success.
- Every time you say thank you, you are a success.
- Every time you sing a happy song, you are a success.

Chapter 9

> A shopkeeper once complained to Rav Moshe of Kobrin that his neighbor, who sold exactly the same goods as he did, always did well, while he could barely manage.
>
> "I can promise a generous income to you, too," said the tzaddik," but only on condition that when you see your neighbor making a profit, you thank Hashem for his success. Something like this: "Blessed is Hashem, Who gives such a good livelihood to a fellow Jew." It may be difficult to say this wholeheartedly at first, but as you train your mouth to say the words, with time they will find their way into your heart as well. For, in the verse, בְּפִיךָ וּבִלְבָבְךָ לַעֲשׂתוֹ, (Devarim 30:14) — in your mouth, and in your heart, that you may do it — we first find the words 'in your mouth,' and only later is it written 'in your heart.' "

(*A Treasury of Chassidic Tales — Devarim*)

Why Is Everything So Difficult?

❧ Question

*T*hings just aren't going well. I can't concentrate. I feel lonely. I feel that I've reached a low point and I don't know how to get out of it. It seems to me that the other students have so many positive capabilities while I have so many faults. If I'm not that talented, is there no hope for me?

❧ Answer

I feel your pain. In school you are among friends who are all pursuing the same goal and listening to the same lessons. In class when every student asks questions and offers answers, each student's talents are revealed. At the same time that talents come forth, limitations are uncovered.

You look at your friends:
This one has a phenomenal memory — and you forget.
This once catches on quickly — and you learn at a slower pace.
If you don't have a good memory and a quick mind, what do you have?

✒ Know Your Strengths

When you work hard to understand something, you may understand it with greater depth. Your friend with the quick mind may understand things only superficially. Your friend with the great memory won't feel the happiness in accomplishment that you do because of the effort you invest in learning.

You tend to see only what you don't have and what others do have. Going to school every day pushes these thoughts to the forefront. Each day you see strengths and weaknesses — your friend's capabilities and your faults. Then one day you feel that you have nothing — no talent, no success, no hope.

Every person has some faults and some talents. The feeling that you **only** have faults while others are flawless is called jealousy. Perhaps it will comfort you to know that every young person suffers from jealousy.

What can you do to overcome your jealousy?

Your job is to recognize that Hashem has given you many qualities and talents that are uniquely yours. You have to become aware that your portion in the universe awaits you alone. No one can accomplish your purpose in life instead of you. Don't measure yourself against your friends' yardsticks. Trust that Hashem has given you the spiritual attributes that you need.

Each morning when you say the blessing — שֶׁעָשָׂה לִי כָּל צָרְכִּי — you thank Hashem for giving you everything you need to accomplish the task Hashem designed for you in the world. Hashem gave you the talent, the emotional strength, and the physical means to achieve the goals He set for you.

You have the attributes you need to receive your portion in the Torah (Adapted from *Sefer Alei Shur*).

✍ Keep on Climbing up

Hashem doesn't give you what you need only once. Hashem gives you new spiritual strength *every* day. Yesterday you were given what you needed to succeed yesterday, and today for today. Every day Hashem helps you grow into what you should be.

Have you ever gone to the eye doctor to have your eyes checked? The doctor uses a contraption that looks like strange eyeglasses. He pulls lenses off the wall and slides them into this contraption. Then he asks you to read the eye chart.

At first you tell him, "No, that lens doesn't help. It's still blurry." The doctor tries another one. Perhaps then you say, "This one is worse than the last one was." Finally, he finds the lens that works. This time you say, "It's clear now. I can see the chart," and you read all the letters on the chart confidently.

In the same way, every one of your attributes and talents fits your soul perfectly. Just as someone else's glasses won't help you see better, someone else's traits won't help you accomplish your mission in life. Your goal is not to surpass others but rather to be the best that you can be.

✍ Seek Your Goals and They Will Find You

Perhaps you don't know what your talents are yet. Is there a way to find out? If you always dreamed of doing something, does your ambition mean anything or must you be born with a talent for that particular task ?

The Chofetz Chaim explains that if one sincerely is interested to serve Hashem in a specific area, Hashem will give him the talents he needs to succeed in that pursuit.

The Chofetz Chaim (*Parshas Terumah*) explains: We find regarding the building of the *Mishkan* that each person who wanted with his whole heart to create something beautiful for the *Mishkan* was granted wisdom by Hashem so that he knew how to do it.

At first one would go to the place where the vessels were made, watch how it was done and offer to help. Afterwards Hashem gave him wisdom from on High to know how to do the intricate work.

This concept applies to all the good things that people want to do to serve Hashem. Whether one strives to help in holy works or whether one is toiling in Torah learning. If one decides wholeheartedly to pursue knowledge and to find clarity, Hashem will surely put intelligence in his heart.

➳ Use Your Gifts Well

There was a king who distributed bolts of raw silk to his servants. He wanted to test their intelligence. The smartest and most diligent servant sorted the silk into three types; the best, the average, and the inferior. From each type he developed the best-quality cloth. He took the cloth to professional tailors and made luxurious royal clothes in different colors. He wore the clothes when he visited the king; each garment at the proper time and place. The foolish servant used *all* his silk in the way that the wise servant had used his most inferior silk. He sold the entire lot at the first opportunity for less than its true worth and hurried to enjoy the money with good food, drink, and similar trivial pursuits. When the king heard this, he gave the wise servant an important position and he exiled the foolish servant.

Hashem gave us wisdom and knowledge. There is the highest part in which are the sublime, delicate spiritual topics. There is the middle part which contains all the obligations and how to fulfill them at the right time and place. After that, there is the third part which has the issues that relate to daily concerns. Each part of wisdom should be used fully at the right time (*Chovos HaLevavos*, Introduction, page 59).

The key to success is not in being someone else. Everyday, Hashem is giving you the wisdom you need. If you are determined you can use your talents and spiritual gifts well.

2-Minute Tips

1. In any situation, you have many possibles ways to think and react:

   - Self-defeating comparison: "If only I were more like . . ."

     OR

   - Positive, uplifting thought: "What should I do to succeed next time?"

   Why not pick the better one?

2. Cultivate many different interests and hobbies, to find out what you do best.

3. Connect with people who see you as a *total* person. Assume their praise is true and try to live up to it.

My great-aunt Berta lived through the communist nightmare, and lost her husband and her only child, yet she still smiles. As soon as I walk through the door, she plants a kiss on my cheek, tells me how happy she is to see me and how pretty I look (even though I have pimples). She encourages me and listens to me. Somehow after talking to her I feel better about myself. When I ask how she feels, she answers cheerfully, "We have to say *Baruch Hashem.*"   *Rikki N.*

Now I Know!

Finding Your Strengths	Comparing
Learning what you can from every situation.	Ignoring your own learning potential because you are measuring yourself against your friend's yardstick.
Striving to be the best **you** that you can be.	Wanting to be like everyone else.
Enthusiastically serving Hashem in many ways.	Hesitating to act, while watching others and thinking, "I could have done that."
Leaning into life.	Pulling away from life.

Chapter 10

" Rav Baruch Mordechai of Warsaw had an open house for anyone who wished to enter. He, too, came and went just like the others. He had no special place at the head of the table.

Once a poor man innocently turned to R' Baruch Mordechai and asked, "I see that you are a steady guest here. Tell me, do you think that they would mind if I stayed here a few weeks longer?"

R' Baruch Mordechai shrugged his shoulders, "No. I am sure you are welcome here. I have been living here — eating and sleeping — for a long time and no one has ever said anything. . ." "

(Tales of Tzaddikim)

Your Friends: The Courage To Reach Out

Baila Gross felt shy in sleep-away camp. She was the only girl from Greenfield in the bunk. Each day she promised herself that she'd start talking to Leah, but she never did. "I wish I could be Leah's friend." Baila thought, "I just know that we're the same type."

Baila felt nervous about approaching Leah because Leah was always with Faigy, the most popular girl in the bunk.

Shyness is a loss for everyone. Who can count the number of kind acts that went undone, the ideas that were never expressed, the helpful life experiences that were never shared because people felt too awkward to act? People suffer alone while others who have been in the same situation could help them, only because both parties hesitate. Gratitude is never expressed and friendships wither and are forever lost.

A crucial Torah thought is that we all have something special to offer the world that no one else can give — ourselves. Think about it for a minute. Physically, people are pretty much alike. We all have two eyes, two hands, two feet. When defining people by their basic character traits, one would find that people are more alike than they are different. Yet, if you have a best friend or a favorite cousin you will feel deep inside, "This person is like no other person alive right now."

What makes that person special and unique? Try right now to describe someone you love —

_____

_____

_____

Why is it so difficult? Because it's not their physical attributes that make them who they really are but their *neshamos*. Each person's *neshamah* is purely spiritual, a part of Hashem, and therefore like no other.

Rav Shlomo Wolbe said:

> *THERE WILL NEVER BE ANOTHER YOU. There has never been someone exactly like you and there will never be another you until the end of time. Every person must remember: "I am a distinct individual with a precise combination of talents. I was born to these parents at this interval in history and in this particular place. Certainly G-d assigned a specific task to me. I have a special portion in Torah. The entire world is waiting for me. No other person in the world can accomplish my mission in life."*
>
> (*Alei Shur,* Harav Shlomo Wolbe, page 168)

During the third week of camp, Faigy left for her brother's *Bar Mitzvah Shabbos.* Baila looked towards Leah and noticed her smile. That small gesture was enough to give Baila the courage to start being friendlier.

During Shabbos Baila and Leah found they had a lot of common hobbies and they even liked the same foods. Leah said, "I wish we had found each other before. I was feeling so lonely this summer in camp."

"You, lonely!" Baila exclaimed. "I thought that since you were with the popular crowd, you wouldn't even look at me." Leah frowned. "Maybe I should be grateful to Faigy. She was nice to me but she always made me feel that it's just because we are cousins. I never felt that she likes me for myself. You like me for myself."

When we stifle who we are, our existence and our world are diminished. We also lose by what others could have contributed had they not been afraid. One key to the willingness to help someone else is to understand how vital a *mitzvah* this is. It is simply one of the keys to our being here today.

❧ Where to Start

I really believe that everyone dreams of reaching out. Everyone cares about those who are feeling left out. Even the popular girls feel like a fish out of water when they are in strange surroundings. They notice that everyone seems to be standing in groups while they stand alone. We can all feel uncomfortable at a family gathering where everyone is either much older or much younger than us. We all know that feeling of insecurity, yet when we see someone else having the same difficulty we feel awkward about approaching them. We're afraid that we will just make the situation worse.

Most of the obstacles to reaching out to others are in our minds. A positive attitude can help us find the courage to take that first step and many times the results will be much better than our best expectation. Some specific things we can do to improve our attitudes about breaking the ice are:

- Think about what you like to do and with whom.
- Give people the benefit of the doubt.
- Have optimistic expectations.
- Don't assume you alone want to be friendly.
- Know that "every little bit helps."

Do you think that a good friendship is supposed to develop instantly? Do you expect that you will meet someone who just thinks you're terrific and from then on you will always do everything together? Most friendships don't just happen all at once.

Sometimes a little thing that you do with a friend grows, like a small seed, into a strong and vibrant relationship.

I was at a wedding last week when a stranger approached me with the standard question, "Were you invited from the *chassan's* side or the *kallah's* side?" Then the *chassan's* aunt turned around and said, "Don't you know who she is? She's Goldie's *chavrusah* (learning partner)."

At 9:15 every morning, instead of diving into the housework, I go to the phone and call my friend Goldie. We both reach for our copies of *Gateway to Happiness,* by Rabbi Zelig Pliskin. For five minutes a day for six months now, we have taken turns reading a paragraph or two and sharing our feelings.

When we finish a paragraph, one of us usually comments, "Wow!" Then there is a quiet pause, and the other invariably says, "That reminds me of something that happened last week . . ."

We could each learn on our own, but it wouldn't be the same. The words of the *sefer* have a deeper meaning when they are shared, and are remembered longer. The partnership also provides a stronger impetus for taking action. Sharing our experiences each day makes the crucial difference between wishful dreaming and actual doing.

Goldie and I didn't know each other at all. We have become close through our daily contact in Torah learning. Whenever I feel overwhelmed, I know I can talk things over with her. Then we began to spend our days off doing things together. Afterwards we began sharing in our children's *simchos.*

School is also a vital place for giving others the benefit of the doubt. When someone seems aloof, he or she may be just as anxious as you are. Even people who have walked away probably didn't mean to hurt you; they just had to rush off and didn't know how to do it better. In the lunchroom the person telling you that a seat is reserved might feel just as uncomfortable as you do; that person will never be forgiven by the girl who sits behind them if that seat is given away.

At times you and your friends will agree. You will both want to do the same things in the same way. Other times you won't agree. It isn't always easy for friends to decide how they should do things when they are together.

Suppose for example that you are working on a school project. Everyone has to agree on what kind of song to compose and what form the model will take. There may be a few opinions.

When you do things by yourself, you can do them your own way. You only have to worry about your ideas and you can make your own decisions.

However when the group works together, your friends might want to do things differently. When you try hard to do things your way while your friends want to do things the other way, you and your friends can get angry at each other. During those times it's important to be flexible and acknowledge that although there is a strong possibility that you are right, it's also equally possible that your friend is right. Compromise is necessary to arrive at a friendly resolution.

The Fifty-Fifty Principle

Rebbitzin Avner mentioned in a lecture that she remembered going to her father, a *Dayan*, when she had a disagreement with a friend when she was eight. She thought that since her father resolved disagreements for others, he could help her and he would surely take her side. Her father said, "If you and your friend have conflicting opinions, there is a very good chance that you are right. Isn't there a chance, however, that your friend is right too? Since there are two of you, let's say that we divide the odds. There is a 50 percent chance that you are right and a 50 percent chance that your friend is right."

Mrs. Avner said, "Since then, I've looked at many difficult situations in life that way, and it helped me see that there were other points of view."

- Can you decide to be open to other opinions and ideas?
- Can you figure out how to consider others and use their ideas?
- Can you wait before giving your opinion?
- Can you accept the idea that sometimes someone else is right too?

If you can learn how to listen to others respectfully, and if you can state your ideas and feelings patiently and without shouting you will be able to learn many new ideas from your friends and in turn you will be much more successful.

> Why did Beis Hillel merit that the Halachah is according to their rule? Because they were patient and tolerant. Whenever they studied Halachah they would consider the opinion of Beis Shammai before their own.

Giving the benefit of the doubt is sometimes the only way that people of different backgrounds can bridge the gap. When I finished a year of study in Israel and was leaving for America, my roommate who lives in Israel gave me a *sefer* that I still treasure and use. Her inscription on the flap was, "At year's end a sweet taste remains in the mouth."

She was referrring to the pleasant memories that she would store and hide away for future use. I was pleased that she was a friend who had always taken the time to savor the caring times we had spent together. I was especially grateful to her for choosing to forget all the differences we struggled with at first. When you share a room with someone there are many adjustments to make, besides dealing with a different language and a different culture. She was meticulously neat and careful while I was too absorbed in my books to care. We wanted to go to sleep at different times and while I had another American girl in the room, she was the only Israeli.

Anyone trying to coordinate a project of any size must have optimistic expectations. If you will successfully ask someone for advice, ideas, help, or money (the hardest?), you must feel enthusiastic first. Yours just might be the call they were waiting for. At the same time be ready to forgive when someone refuses. They may have a really good reason that you discover afterwards.

It can be hard to share your feelings and it can be hard to wait for someone to reciprocate a favor — even with friends. When you share your feelings and give to others without expecting them to immediately repay you, you are being a good friend.

Consequently, our Sages advise in *Pirkei Avos* 1:6, קְנֵה לְךָ חָבֵר, *buy a friend* (literally, קְנֵה means *buy;* the intention is to *acquire*). Friends have to be "bought" sometimes. Occasionally *you* have to take the initiative and give. *You* have to give your attention, your time, your smile, and your heart. You can't just wait for the other person to make the first move. If you are optimistic, it will be easier for you to give.

"As water reflects one face to another face, so too is one heart to another heart" (*Mishlei* 27:19). What one friend feels about another, the other feels. If you view your friend positively, he or she will regard you positively. If you view your friend negatively, he or she will harbor the same feelings about you.

וֶהֱוֵי מְקַבֵּל אֶת כָּל הָאָדָם בְּסֵבֶר פָּנִים יָפוֹת, *And greet every person with a cheerful expression on your face (Avos* 1:16). Rabbi Yitzchok of Vorki asks: Why do we need the word סֵבֶר (expression) here?

When in your heart you don't have pleasant feelings toward the other person, but you express good cheer and smile at that person, when someone comes to visit at an inconvenient time and you welcome him or her with patience and good cheer — this is a very good character trait.

The Rebbe of Vorki is telling us that even when we don't feel it, we should pretend that we are happy and we will be able to convince others and help them feel better.

Don't assume that you are the only one who wants to be friendly. It is quite frustrating to carry on a one-sided conversation or to greet someone who barely mumbles an answer. Yet many times those people are anxious and shy. It's only after you become close friends that you find out just how relieved the other person was that you were the one to break the ice.

On the first day of first grade I nervously walked into the classroom and encountered a group of strange faces. I swiftly crawled into my chair, hoping that no one had seen me. When the teacher asked a question, I quickly tried to answer so everyone would think I was smart and would want me for a friend.

At recess I realized I was not the only one without any friends. It was the first day for everyone. Shyly I walked over to one girl and asked her quietly if she want to play a game. I received a quiet stare. I assumed she didn't want to play so I went over to the next girl. The first girl looked after me solemnly. She had really wanted to play but she felt too shy.

I asked the second girl to play and all I got was the same stare. Thinking that I must be the weird one, I quietly sat down in my seat.

The years passed. Those same two girls were always in my class. And we still gave each other those solemn looks.

One day in sixth grade a teacher assigned a journal topic: Write about something that happened that you wish you could change. The teacher read some of the compositions out loud. One of them seemed to be by the girl who gave me the stare in the first grade. She wrote about how she regretted that moment. She lost a friend she hoped to have.

At recess that day we both hesitantly walked over to each other and made up for the first six years.

Now we are inseparable friends.   *C.R.*

When I was recently at a *Tzedakah* party someone sat near me who spoke only Hebrew. I wanted to speak to her in Hebrew, a language that I know fluently, yet I felt uncomfortable about the situation at first. How will I carry on two conversations at once? After several minutes I decided that I must take the initiative and speak to my neighbor in Hebrew. Once I began, I found that it wasn't as awkward as I had supposed. Everyone at the table chose to follow my example and speak Hebrew too, although perhaps not as fluently as I. It turned out that I wasn't the only one who wanted to be friendly.

When you have been close with someone for a while, is it sometimes hard to let someone else join your group? You might be afraid that your friends will decide that they like the new person better. Perhaps you wonder if you will be as close as before if someone new joins in. As the saying goes, "Two is company but three is a crowd." Friends don't have to be together all the time. It can be a good feeling to know that you can have many friends. Letting someone who is lonely join you when you do something together is a tremendous *chesed*. Sometimes we don't realize how important it is.

> *There is now abundant evidence to show that social support may be one of the critical elements distinguishing those who remain healthy from those who do not. Social support works to prevent illness by protecting the immune system. Positive and supportive associations, such as community support and close friends or family, have been linked to better health and the resulting lower absenteeism, lower incidence of cancer and heart disease, reduced hospital stays, better health*

in married persons versus singles, increased resistance to streptococcal infection, and increased resistance to Epstein- Barr virus among an entire West Point Cadet Class followed over four years.

(Preface, *Mind as Healer, Mind as Slayer,* Kenneth R. Pelletier, p. 48).

How can you welcome an outsider into your group?

Perhaps when you are planning to get together with friends, you can invite someone who is lonely. Or if you are going somewhere special, you can ask someone new to come along. You can study together for a test or go together to do a *chesed.* Even sharing your snack not just with your friends, but with someone who looks lonely, can make an outsider feel a lot better.

Exercise

Have you ever welcomed an outsider into your group? What were the results?

_____

_____

_____

Actual Responses

"When I was a 10th grader I came to study in a high school in New York from out of town. I've always made friends easily, so after a while I developed a circle of friends who I'm still close with today. The circle is always growing. I'm always making new friends and introducing them to my old friends. I will never allow someone else to feel left out if I can help them. I know how it feels not to know anyone; not even to have family nearby."

Leah said, "This happened while we were making seating arrangements for my brother's *bar-mitzvah*. There was an Orthodox woman who worked as a housekeeper and babysitter for my mother."

My mother wondered, "Where do we sit Mrs. Borochov? She doesn't know anyone but the immediate family."

My aunt said, "I would like her to sit next to me."

"But you are supposed to be at the head table," my mother said to my aunt.

"Well, she must sit next to me and I don't mind where I'll be sitting. I don't want her to feel embarrassed," my aunt responded.

My mother was impressed. "I never knew that this lady means so much to you."

"You don't understand," my aunt replied. " I came here from Hungary in 1949. This babysitter came to America in 1990. Thank G-d, I was able to escape the communist countries earlier and to build up a successful life in America. That doesn't make me any better, only luckier. I was also "a greener.""

When I was in Neve Yerushalayim I had a wonderful roommate. We were compatible in many aspects and I learned a lot from her. Suddenly the administration decided to put someone who had walked into the Seminary "off the street" into the apartment. While we had accepted many *mitzvos* already and dressed modestly, this girl knew almost nothing and wore shorts and sandals. We feared that she'd make our pots and dishes *treif.*

The principal encouraged us, "Give it a week. If you see that she isn't into this lifestyle, we'll put her into a regular dormitory apartment. I think that if you are friendly you can really help this girl."

We invited her to join us for pizza and other social events. One day she commented, "You live so normally yet you are religious. I had never thought you could be a Torah observer and be a normal person too. Don't you feel restricted?"

My religious roommate answered, "I can do everything that I want to do. Being religious helps me. When I'm out in Manhattan shopping and I think over my choices of what I can eat, I'll pick a banana from a fruit stand. I won't crave fattening ice cream because it's not kosher. I like to wear skirts, I don't look good in shorts. Being religious also solves many of my day-to-day practical decisions. I am at peace with things that bog down most of another person's day, so now I can spend my time thinking about more important things."

The girl we had welcomed into our apartment did eventually become religious and lives in Israel. Her husband is studying to become a rabbi. She has three beautiful children.

In our neighborhood, whenever a new family moves in we make a party on Friday night. Last time 20 neighbors came to meet the new girl who had just moved in on my block. We all spent time getting to know the new girl and emphasizing that we were all here for her whenever she needs us. Do you want to join our neighborhood? I'd love to have your family on our block. I'm looking forward to another Friday night party.

While I was sitting in my classroom, my eyes darted across the room and landed on the new girl. "What a nice girl," I thought. That night I was on the phone with my best friend. I mentioned this girl to her. The next day my teacher put up a new seating chart and I got a seat near the new girl.

"Hi! Do you want to come over to my house on Sunday to study?" she asked.

"Well, I already made plans to study with my friend, but I guess we could all study together," I answered.

After we decided that all three of us would study together at the new girl's house, that was all she talked about all week. Finally on Sunday we got together. We were talking more than studying at first, but after a while we all buckled down to study. We were all having such a good time.

Since that Sunday the three of us have met every Shabbos. We have become such good friends. We trust each other. We can have fun and sad times together. We like each other the way we are.   *Nechoma S.*

While Surie, Gitty, and I were standing together discussing school I noticed Leah standing to a side. She was new in school and new in the neighborhood. I walked over to Leah. A smile lit up her face — someone had noticed her at last. As we spoke I realized she was very intelligent and also shy. I took down her phone number.

At first she was too shy to come to my house so I went to her house. Soon she felt more comfortable with me. Then I started pulling her into my circle of friends. After a while we felt like Leah had been with us forever.   *Shaindy G.*

On Friday afternoon, shortly before Shabbos, the bell rang. I ran to the door. Our usual Shabbos guest had brought along a girl with curly red hair. "This is my daughter," he said. She wore short sleeves, pants, and bright red high-top sneakers. We welcomed them in, made them comfortable and left further discussion for later. I loaned her one of my Shabbos dresses. When she came downstairs she stared wide eyed as my mother lit the Shabbos candles.

After the meal she told us her story. "My parents are divorced, as you know. My older sister and I chose to live with our mother in another part of the city. We lead a completely different lifestyle. We don't keep Shabbos, kosher, or even the holidays. We're real American girls. My mother has a terrible temper and the situation in our house is terrible. This morning I told my sister that I can't handle this anymore and want to go to our father. I asked her to come with me. She tried to discourage me, but I was determined. I called my father and asked if I could come to him and here I am."

That Shabbos my sister introduced her to a lot of her friends. We all tried to give her a big welcome. On *Motzaei Shabbos* my sister contacted a teacher who she thought could answer some of her questions.

She began coming to us most *Shabbosos* and every single *Yom Tov*. Two years later she married a *frum* boy. My father made the *shidduch*. Our family made a beautiful *Sheva Brachos*. Her new friends that she had met over the last two years all joined in the *simchah*.

Today her home looks just like ours. She barely resembles the stranger that stood at our door that Friday afternoon.

Estie Z.

A Good Word

It may seem obvious to many of you to give a compliment or an encouraging word. After all, it doesn't cost anything to be nice. You may not think it is necessary to even bring these examples. However, being careful with our speech is essential, for two reasons. First, it is emphasized repeatedly by our Sages. For example, הַמְקַבֵּל אֶת חֲבֵרוֹ בְּסֵבֶר פָּנִים יָפוֹת אֲפִילוּ לֹא נָתַן לוֹ כְּלוּם מַעֲלֶה עָלָיו הַכָּתוּב כְּאִלוּ נָתַן לוֹ כָּל מַתָּנוֹת טוֹבוֹת שֶׁבָּעוֹלָם, *One who welcomes his friend with a caring and smiling face and a cheerful greeting, although he gave him nothing more, is considered as though he has given him all the good gifts of this world* (*Avos D'Rav Nosson*).

The second reason is that nothing has ruined more friendships than a thoughtless remark. The hurt person feels, "If she could say a thing like that after all I have done for her and all that we've shared, I just can't feel the same way about her anymore. What does it cost her to be caring?"

Dina said, "I know what you mean. A school friend of mine called me for help. I spent hours getting her help from various organizations to ease her plight. I got everything from reduced medical care to a nice Shabbos dress for her. We spoke every day and I listened to each day's problems and I tried to encourage her. Then several months later something really devastating happened to me. We met and I wanted to talk to her about it and hear her opinion. As I explained the situation, I noticed that she was doing other things. In frustration, I exclaimed, 'This is really important, can't you listen?' She replied 'OK, let's hear about your silly problem.' If she calls I will still help her, but the feeling inside just isn't the same."

One morning, after *Shacharis,* a woman entered, crying pitifully. She was a widow. Her daughter was in labor, suffering an unusually difficult delivery, with both mother and infant in danger. The widow begged Reb Baruch Ber to say *Tehillim* on their behalf and to pray for their welfare. He fulfilled her request with much feeling and tears filled his eyes. Before leaving, she handed the *Rosh Yeshivah* some money wrapped up in newspaper as a donation for the *Yeshivah.* I glanced into the scrap of paper. It only held several pennies, hardly enough to buy two loaves of bread! Reb Baruch Ber carried the paper containing the money to the stairs, calling: "Reuvain! Please hurry! A lady brought money for the *yeshivah,* come take it!" It was clear that he wanted to impress the widow with his gratitude.

There was a woman who so admired Rabbi Aryeh Levin that she took pains to knit him a pair of woolen gloves. When she brought them to him, however, he refused to accept them. "How," Reb Aryeh explained, "will I be able to feel a person's hand when he holds it out to me in friendly greeting?"

(*A Tzaddik in Our Time,* p. 352)

I call my friend every *Motzaei Shabbos* to wish her a good week. Here is an excerpt from her letter that describes how she feels about our weekly calls.

"It was short. Our conversation tonight was short, but it was just perfect. We were waving to each other, sharing a smile, throwing a kiss and then back to our duties in life. Each finding strength in those few moments. I remember how you said, 'When I smile now here in Monsey, can you feel it in Flatbush? Can you hear me laugh with you?' "

I call my great-aunt every Friday to wish her a good Shabbos and to ask how she is feeling. We chat for a short while. She has mentioned several times that she is happy that I remember her.

2-Minute Tips
How Can You Be a Friend?

While waiting with your baby sister on your front porch on Shabbos, a girl about your age whom you haven't met walks by.

From the following choices, what would you do?

A. I'd feel too shy to do anything, but I'd smile.

B. I'd call out, "Good Shabbos." I'd also tell this girl a little about myself and how long I'm in the neighborhood. When the other girl introduces herself I'd repeat her name and make an effort to remember it. If we would meet again I'd make sure to stop and talk.

C. I'd wave and nod my head and hope the other person greets me first.

D. I'd run inside to check my outfit to be sure that I look presentable. I'd also fix my barrette.

The best choice would be B. You would make your neighbor happy, and she would remember that there's a nice person living on her block. Later, it would be easier to establish a closer friendship. If you absolutely couldn't bring yourself to follow B, C at least is a polite gesture.

Rabbi Yochanan ben Zakai taught, "Be the first to greet every person." When we follow this advice we bring a lot of blessing into our life.

Now I Know!

- I know that I need to step forward and be friendly. I can do a kind act, talk about my feelings, and share with others.

- I can listen to others respectfully. I can state my ideas and feelings patiently.

- Best friends don't have to be together all the time. I can have many friends. Letting someone who is lonely join us when we do something together is a tremendous *chesed*.

Chapter 11

"*Heaven is kind to all who are kind to their fellow man. One who does acts of kindness will receive love from Hashem. He will receive it to the extent that he engages in it.*"

(*Mesillas Yesharim, Chelkai Chassidus, page 229*)

Caring and Sharing

*S*ometimes we wonder if just being there for someone really makes a difference. That was the question that Zahava expressed in a letter she sent me.

"Two years ago my friend's father passed away. She felt very close to me and told me all her problems. A year after her father passed away, her mother remarried. This changed her life very much. She changed schools the next year. Although we go to different schools we still keep in touch. She still comes over and fills me in on her latest problems.

"All this puts me in a strange position. I never know what to say because I was *Baruch Hashem* never in her place. However, I always listen. Sometimes it makes things hard for me. I promised I wouldn't share what my friend tells me with

154 □ A HAPPIER YOU

anyone, but I need to talk about this too. I feel that my feelings are bottled up inside.

"Another problem is that she has a habit of talking about me and saying things that aren't true. I can't tell her anything because I know she's just saying these things for attention. I don't want to hurt her. Her life is hard enough already.

"I know I could get out of this problem because we go to different schools now. If I am helping by caring and listening, it pays to continue the friendship. If I can't solve her problems anyway, do the little things I can do make a difference?"

Through the thousands of years of exile, hardship and wandering, Jews have demonstrated their faith in Hashem and their loyalty to the ideals of the Torah by caring for each other and helping each other. Deep down, Jews understand that we are one huge family. When we help our fellow Jew, we don't become weaker, we only become stronger. This tradition continues.

I came into my parents' home and found my mother at her desk in the living room holding an invitation to a *Tzedakah* party, which was dedicated in honor of a close relative. My mother read the invitation aloud and said, "Write down the date. You really must come. This woman probably saved hundreds of people during the Holocaust."

My mother was thoughtful for a moment. "If I had a knack for speaking I'd have a lot to say. Our generation is getting older and soon our experiences during the war years will be lost. Do you know about this woman, for instance? They were very wealthy and they loaded two wagons with the family and the barest necessities along with some gold and silver that they might be able to barter in the future in order to survive. They left everything else behind — their home, furniture, beautiful clothes, china, and the rest of their silver — none of that mattered anymore.

"As they rode toward the Russian border they passed other Jews who had no wagons and were fleeing on foot. With each mile they covered, they picked up passengers. How did they have room? They threw their possessions away and left them on the road in order to squeeze in more people.

"One of the last things they kept was a small bassinet. They needed it because Mrs. Wolf was expecting a child and, without the bassinet, where could they keep the tiny infant? Finally they threw the bassinet onto the highway as well, for Mrs. Wolf said, 'A human life is more important.'

"In the end they were left with nothing, not even the warm blankets and clothing they would surely need in Russia. They threw everything away to save another life.

"I am sure that the true dignity of the Jewish nation came out during those terrible times. The friendship and caring that Jews showed for each other gave us the will to endure for another day. I'm sure that none of us could have survived the war or built up families, schools, *shuls,* and other community institutions if we hadn't been really devoted friends to each other.

"When Germany attacked Poland, I was forced to run away. I was 18 years old and I never saw my parents again. Many others were all alone like I was. We had no support system and lived in constant fear. What was our focus? What gave us hope? It was friendship. Sometimes someone you had never met before would sacrifice his or her last possession to help you. Another time when you felt desperate you had to continue, because someone else depended on you for survival. It was this that gave us hope, faith in the future and the will to survive."

≈⊙ Beauty in the Bottomless Pit

The Hero Who Returned the Slice of Bread

If we start to count the heroic deeds of individual Jews we may never finish. In fact, why even bother to look for isolated instances of Jewish courage and self-sacrifice? Every hungry Jew was the greatest of heroes! Every day and every moment the hungry Jew, who did not forget he was a Jew, was a hero. Hunger can make a person lose his mind and forget his Maker. "The victims of the sword were better off than the victims of hunger," the lamenter has said in his lamentation. Does anyone know the meaning of the insanity of hunger better than us, who have experienced it? Does anyone know better than us the longing for a slice of bread?

I don't know if any other language in the world has an equivalent to the Hebrew expression cherpas ra'av, the disgrace of hunger. . . Hunger is a disgrace . . . It causes not only physical pain, but it also degrades. It enslaves all of the senses and all of the thoughts. One dreams of food constantly, whether awake or asleep. One talks about nothing else, and fights over small bits of food with his friends. . .

Go and learn, how great the faith of the Jews was! Hunger and faith, after all, are opposites! Hunger degrades the soul and makes the body master over it. It puts matter over spirit. But the Jews in the camp knew how to overcome their hunger and remembered that they were Jews. Without a strong faith one would not have been able to keep his bread ration until evening. And many did! I was one of them. The whole thing might have been a matter of conditioning. Only once, only the first time, was difficult. The second time was much easier. It paid to leave the ration. A small piece of bread could save a life. There were some weaker ones among us, who could not save up their ration until evening, and at night they were starved. There were those who shared their bread in the evening with a weak Jew. I did it myself more than once. I didn't look upon it as a great sacrifice. What difference did it make? If you were going to die that night, at least you have saved a fellow Jew on your last day. And if not, if you got up in the morning to go to work, you were like a newly born and you had new hope. . .

"Israel is a holy people!" Satan wanted to turn our

bread into idol worship, Heaven forbid. But the Jews resisted and prevailed! Here is an incident in which I myself was involved.

One evening I was summoned by the camp commander. I knew what it meant. Everyone was prepared for this. I immediately settled my account with my Maker. I made silent confession. I still had my entire bread ration. What use was it now? I said goodbye to my neighbors and divided my worldly possessions among them. This was how we used to do it. I took off my warm coat, and I exchanged my shoes for an old, torn pair. I left, but my luck smiled upon me and I immediately returned. The murderer must have been too lazy to deal with me, and he sent me back to the cabin. When I entered the cabin everyone was surprised. They all returned my belongings. I remembered my bread ration. After all, I was alive and I was still enslaved to that idolatry . . . My neighbor got up and gave me back my bread. He gave me the whole thing. He didn't even want to keep some for himself. He didn't want to. He returned the entire ration. He was happy I was alive. He was truly happy, you could see it in his face. The courage of a Jew! The moral courage!

(*Sparks of Glory*, Moshe Prager, pp. 145-147)

The Fifteenth of Shevat

Two days later, Hugo Gross also received a parcel, from the wife of his former German employer. She sent him some clothing and food, including three rosy apples. I remember them particularly, because on consulting my handwritten calendar I found that the day the package arrived was the 15th of Shevat, celebrated as the New Year of Trees when it is traditional to eat a large variety of fruit — if possible, fifteen kinds.

At my suggestion, Gross cut his three apples into tiny

portions and offered them to each of us at the "religious table," giving us a chance to make the traditional blessing on fruit. It was a kindly act on Hugo's part to share his apples so unselfishly with his friends. To this very day Hugo, who now lives in Jerusalem, receives every 15th of Shevat a huge parcel of fruit containing at least fifteen varieties of fruit from his camp colleague, Gestetner, who now lives in New York, in appreciation and recognition of that day in Nieder Orschel.

(*The Yellow Star,* Simcha Bunem Unsdorfer, p. 159)

What do you do when someone you know has a problem that is too big to solve? Sometimes people run away when they see a friend in trouble. They are afraid of a problem they cannot solve. They feel cut off from the person in trouble. They feel sorry for him or her but they don't know what to do.

We have to know that even the little things we do can make a difference. A person with a big problem is still a person with *many* needs. Don't think of their problem as separate. They need help in many ways, on many levels — not only in ways directly related to the problem at hand. When you connect with someone in a crisis by making a small gesture, you are helping that person on a deeper level as well. Malka Yehudis describes the pain of loneliness below:

I squirmed under her scrutinizing eyes. She expected a mechanical answer to her seemingly simple question. What could I do? I couldn't lie and I'd have to answer sometime.

"I can't understand why you're thinking so much." She interrupted my thoughts. "It's a simple question and not in any way personal."

"That's what you think." I reflected silently. "It might be impersonal for many girls, but not for me. There's no question I dread as much as this one.'

I blushed again under her prying stare. What was I supposed to answer?

"It seems you misunderstood my question," she remarked. "All I asked was who are your friends."

Left with no choice I stared at the ground and mumbled, "Nobody." *Malka Yehudis Z.*

I realized the importance of little kind acts when I visited a bungalow colony several summers ago. Some of the women had organized a Chinese auction to raise money for a free loan fund in the memory of young man who had recently passed away after a serious illness. His young widow stood up to thank everyone for coming. She said, "I will never forget a cup of coffee someone brought to me on Shabbos morning when I was in the hospital near my husband's bedside. That person had to go down eight flights of stairs to the cafeteria and back up another eight flights to bring me the coffee. That cup of coffee still warms my insides today because it showed me that I'm not alone and that people care."

There is constant communication between us and Hashem. It's not only when we talk to Hashem that we tell Him what we want. A powerful message is sent through our actions. Through the little gestures of caring we make it possible for great and good things to come to the world. As Ben Azzai said in *Pirkei Avos* 4:2, הֱוֵי רָץ לְמִצְוָה קַלָּה . . . שֶׁשְּׂכַר מִצְוָה מִצְוָה, *Run to perform even a 'minor' mitzvah because the reward (consequence) of a mitzvah is a mitzvah.*

How was Moses chosen to lead the Jewish nation out of Egypt? He was living in the king's palace and Pharaoh's daughter gratified his wishes but he remembered that he was a Jew. The Torah says, וַיֵּצֵא אֶל אֶחָיו וַיַּרְא בְּסִבְלֹתָם, *He went out to his brothers and observed their burdens* (*Shemos* 2:11). The Sages (*Shemos Rabbah*) explain further, "Moses was weeping, 'I feel so much pain over your difficult work.' He helped one person after another carry the heavy rocks. He put down his walking stick and sat with them at their workplace. He spoke to his Jewish brothers and realized that they have no rest. So he approached Pharaoh and said, "You will benefit if you give your slaves a day of rest. They will live longer and be more productive. Pharaoh agreed to give them a day of rest. Moshe went and established the Shabbos day as their day of leisure."

When Hashem saw that Moshe cared and tried in every way to alleviate the plight of his brothers, He declared, "You, Moses, will lead them out of Egypt."

When Moshe first saw the misery of his Jewish brothers, could he make them into free men? No, but he did not give up. He did what he could to help. Thereby he merited to be the messenger of God when the time came to take the Jewish nation out of Egypt.

The *mitzvah* of "Nichum Aveilim," comforting the bereaved, conveys this important point. The *Halachah* gives us a framework for approaching someone in great pain. Everyone who knows the person can go and offer to show they care. You can bring food, leave *Tzedakah* for the departed's memory, speak a few words, listen a lot and offer a prayer that they can hear: "*HaMakom Yenachem Eschem. . .*"

When Moshe helped the other Jews carry the heavy rocks he showed he was concerned. Every small action of giving is a visible demonstration that you really care about others. A little bit really does help because it shows that you are reaching out and staying in touch.

Don't become paralyzed when you see a problem. You don't have to solve it. You just have to be compassionate and Hashem will do the rest. And in the merit of helping and sharing, may you always be on the giving end.

Exercise

In what way has a friend helped you when you felt you couldn't cope? How have you helped your friend through a difficulty?

_____

_____

Describe a situation where a cycle of kindness began: Your friend did you a favor and later when she needed you, you helped her?

_____

_____

When did your friend help you to do something that was too much for one person alone — school project, tzedakah function. . .?

_____

_____

Have you ever given or received advice from a friend and become closer thereby?

_____

_____

Your Friends' Actual Responses

✍ Help When You Couldn't Cope

When I feel upset, it's good to have someone I can call who can comfort me. My friend also calls me when she is upset, and I can comfort her. I can call my friend to help me with my homework and we can study together before a test.

Without friendship, the world would be very, very lonely. Friendship is precious. Friends have to be appreciated.

Naomi L.

During the *Brachos* Bee, Menucha and I kept looking at each other nervously. We held hands tightly and as we faced the questions. After a while, Menucha said the wrong *berachah* and was out. "Now what will I do without my best friend next to me, holding my hand and whispering, 'Good luck,' on every turn?"

Although my friend was no longer in the competition she helped me study for the final round. She tested me over and over again, until I knew it. I wouldn't have won without my friend's support throughout the *Brachos* Bee. *Elky B.*

My friend helps me by studying with me and helping me with homework. When we have a lot of tests, my friend tries to cheer me up about it. When I'm absent, she takes notes for me. When I'm feeling blue, I call her and she brightens me up.

We do everything together. She always stands by my side. Best of all, when we get into a fight she's the one to settle it. I really owe her a lot. *Meital R.*

She sat by the window, and stared at the cheerful scene outside. The children ran around outside happily drinking in the early spring sunshine. No one stopped to notice her. They were all immersed in their own healthy and joyful lives. I broke apart from my group. I tapped softly on the window, and whispered a shy hello. Her deep dark eyes took on a new shine. They reflected the joy she felt within. *Devorah P.*

A while ago, a classmate of mine lost her mother. I was a good friend of hers. I was inconsolable for a week. That night I was in desperate need for someone to cry to. I called my great friend in Monsey. In a cracking voice I told her the news, and we cried and cried. Instead of just saying, "It'll be all right," she cried also. After we hung up from each other, I felt so much better. *Sara H.*

A Cycle of Kindness

My friend is very special and cannot be replaced. We learn similar subjects so we switch notes. For example, we both learn global history so he gave me his notes on Japan which I am learning. I gave him my notes on China which I learned already. We both take math so we both study together. When it's late at night and I'm bursting to tell a secret, I go and tell my friend who confides in me too. Not too many people have friends like I do because my friend is my twin.

My father is friendly with this family for a long time. At their *Sheva Brachos,* my father did the photography. Since then, at every family celebration of theirs and at every celebration of ours, the families do the photography for one another. My father and his friend are professional photographers and don't ever charge one another for anything — not even the film.

Esther A.

On the first day of camp I should have been lonely and apprehensive, but I wasn't scared because of my good friend Nechy. Nechy always gave me a smile, especially when I needed it most. She was always there to cheer me up. When I needed help composing songs and dances for color war, she was at my side helping me and pulling me through.

I always wished I could somehow let Nechy know how much she meant to me and what a difference she made in my summer. Then I realized how I'd been returning her kindness all summer long. Nechy had a brain tumor removed a while ago. *Baruch Hashem,* she's fine now, but she had to go to the infirmary for shots and medicine. I always accompanied her. At times it was raining or hot and sometimes it was late at night. I always went because I knew my company meant a lot to her.

What's a friendship without *chesed*? *Aviva C.*

Joint Effort

Three years ago I made *Sheva Brachos* for a school friend on a Sunday. I wanted to buy a case of chicken, but it wasn't so easy because I don't drive. I had to have the chicken on Thursday. That Thursday morning it was pouring, and I had no way of getting to the butcher. A friend came with her two babies and took me to pick up the chicken. She also helped me drag the 60 pounds of chicken up the steps and into my house. She had done all her shopping on Wednesday and had no personal reason to go out to shop in the rain that day, but she did it to help me.

Advice

I had never been that close with a girl in my class. Then we started walking home together. We talked as we walked home. Once she asked me for advice on what to tell another girl who had asked her for advice. We came up with a solution together. After that, we always asked each other for advice or help. Now we are very close friends. *Devorah S.*

Once in camp an acquaintance was having problems with another bunkmate. She had a good cry on my shoulder and we had a long discussion. We were never really friendly, but since that night , we have been close friends. *Devorah R.*

2-Minute Tips

1. Strive to express empathy to others in as many ways as you can think of. Sit down right now and make a list of people who are sad or lonely and think of a way you can comfort each one within the next week.

2. Go through your things and find things you don't use very often. Give them to others who will appreciate them more. This past Purim a 12th grader in Monsey urged all the girls in her school to contribute their Purim *Mishloach Manos* candies to be shipped to Russia. Many children in Russia rarely see even one kosher candy and it's a very precious treat for them.

3. If you are a person who always hunts for a bargain, spend a little extra money in a store that just opened. Even if the product costs a few cents more, your small action can give a lot of encouragement to the people who are just starting a new business.

4. Be creative. Think of ways to be kind and encouraging to the younger kids in your family and on your block.

Chapter 12

> One Sunday in the Hermann Goering factory someone remembered that it was Simchas Torah. So he sang at the top of his lungs the "Mi Pi Keil" song.
>
> No one is mighty like G-d, No one is blessed like Moshe, There is no greatness like Torah. No one expounds it like the Jews, There are none as wise as the Jews.
>
> Suddenly we became aware of the chief of our factory in the room, and the singer stopped cold.
>
> "What is going on here? Tell me, Friedenson, what is he singing?" I explained that it was a Jewish holiday.
>
> "But what do the words mean?"
>
> Again I explained.
>
> "Do you really believe that Friedenson?" he asked.
>
> A young fellow prisoner, quite unlearned, jumped to his feet and said, "Yes, I believe!" The German shook his head and muttered, "Unbelievable! I'm afraid that the Fuhrer will never succeed with you people."

(Rabbi Yosef Friedenson)

Peer Pressure: Are You Afraid To Be Different?

I remember this from kindergarten. It was the first day of school. My mother packed my lunch in a big brown bag. When I sat down at the table, I noticed that no one else had a brown bag. I felt so uptight and sensitive. I was sure that everyone was looking at my bag of lunch. It's funny how we worry about what other people will think. Most of the time they aren't thinking about it at all."

"I once found a scrap of paper with a spiteful, insulting note in my purse. That year my friend and I decided that everyone in the class was against us. Since I *didn't know who wrote it, I suspected many of my classmates. I still don't know who wrote that note. To this day, whenever I find a scrap of paper in my purse, my heart jumps."*

"You wouldn't worry so much about what other people thought if you realized how seldom they do."
                                        Eleanor Roosevelt

"I wanted to tell you an interesting conversation that I had with Leah in America. 'I'll tell you the truth,' Leah remarked. 'I want to be a serious individual. I want to dress differently and speak differently. I'm not interested in the jokes and gossip and small talk of my friends. I feel uncomfortable in some of the clothes I own. But I'm afraid to be peculiar. I don't want to stand out. I want to be a typical student. I don't want people to point at me and say I'm a rebbetzin or a yente. I don't want to be the one who stands alone. I can't. I can't fight everyone. I want to feel good with the crowd. I'd like to request that you come to my class and talk to them. Perhaps if you meet the class, something will change.' "   (From a tape by Chedva Silberfarb A"H)

I empathize with Leah in Chedva's story. When I had just graduated from seminary, I had a similar struggle. I had just returned to America after studying in *Eretz Yisrael* and I desperately wanted to fulfill all the ideals I had learned about, but I felt that each time I dressed a certain way or said no to *Lashon Hara* I was taking a tremendous risk. Imagined conflicts caused me to become distant from former friends, unnecessarily.

My experience isn't unusual. During a discussion at a lecture at *Shalheves* about developing confidence and courage, many examples were brought.

"We see that the majority of people around us are not into it. It's peer pressure or peer influence. People don't learn the laws of *Lashon Hara* because when they know more they will have to act on this knowledge. When everyone is talking *Lashon Hara* and you keep quiet, you feel weird."

"I have an example. When I was in the bungalow colony, everyone was signing up for the washing machine on the Ninth of Av. I thought it was contrary to the spirit of the day, but I signed up too. I needed a turn at that washing machine."

"I thought of going to a Torah Seminar but I'm a very honest person. If I go, I'll have to change and my friends would think I fell off the moon."

"I agonized over speaking to my cousin who brings inappropriate toys when she comes to visit. Finally, I called last night. I told my cousin in the nicest way I could that the toys she was bringing weren't exactly right for us. She said it was no problem. I gave a few suggestions for appropriate toys. It worked out OK, but I was very frightened to do it."

It seems like this question has no answer. Chedva *A"H* had an answer. I've told her story to many audiences since I heard it and they felt encouraged.

> *I spoke with the class. I told them about a young boy. Some adults saw him playing near a harbor where the ocean liners pass. 'Little boy,' they asked, 'Why are you playing here near the harbor? Go play in the sand like everyone.' The little boy refuses, 'No, I want to stand here. I want to see the big ships. I want to wave hello to the captain.' The adults ask, 'Little boy, don't be silly. Do you really think the captain on the ship will notice you? Go and play with the other children in the sand.'*
> *The young boy stubbornly replies, 'No, I can't go and play there like everyone. I want to stay here. I have to*

*wave hello. Look, I even have a little flag. When I wave
this flag for the captain, the sailors raise all the flags on
the ship and wave back to me.'*

*The people laugh, 'Little boy, that's a silly thing to
say. The captain is busy. He doesn't see your flag. Come
on now, go and play in the sand like everyone else.'*

"*The little boy resists, 'No, I'm positive that when I
wave a salute to the captain that the ship signals back
to me with all the flags.' And the adults smile, 'Little
boy, you are imagining it. Don't be different, play with
the others.' The little boys says, 'No, I have to wave my
flag. I'm sure the captain will pay attention. I'm positive
that the ship notices me. The captain of the ship is my
father. We developed this signal. When I wave my little
flag, my father waves back with all the flags on the
ship.'*

"*When the people hear this they reconsider. 'Maybe
we were foolish after all. The captain is his father.
Surely a father sees and cares.'*

"*When someone asks us, 'Girls, why do you dress
differently? Why do you act differently?' we can say,
"Hashem is our Father. He sees us.' "*

(*Chedva Silberfarb A"H*)

Sara *Emeinu* was also called Yiskah. Yiskah is derived from
the root סָכָה, *to see*. Our Sages say this name showed two of
Sara *Emeinu's* qualities: סָכָה — All *gazed* at her beauty. סָכָה
— She *saw* deeply with *Ruach Hakodesh* (insight from the
Almighty). My teacher Rabbi Shereshevsky *Z"L* explained. "It
is a special praise to Sara *Emeinu* that she had both qualities
together. Physical beauty and deep interest in spiritual pursuits
are a rare and exquisite combination. Usually if people are
beautiful outside they are so carried away with that, they think
of nothing more."

Shani is beautiful. From her *sheitel's* fringe of wisps to her
shoes, every inch is appropriate (even on weekdays). Her
graceful dark suit is classy but understated. It must be her

radiant smile that makes one think it's easy to look this good. Yet she influences her surroundings with her presence in a deeper, more meaningful way — with a good word to reassure and a kind deed to support. Her happy pride in Torah values is compelling. Harav Emanuel Tehila compared this type of charisma to an overflowing fountain that doesn't run dry. When there is constantly a lot inside, the zest for Torah over-flows and fills everyone nearby.

I like to talk to Shani because she never gossips. When she hears it's me she usually says, "So, Roiza, what's the good word?" I know before I call I have to prepare a Torah thought.

Two years ago when she was in a bungalow colony and I was in the city, I missed our weekly exchange of Torah thoughts, so I called her in Monroe. A five-year-old boy answered the public phone. "You want Edelstein? OK, I'll call her." After five minutes (don't they know this is long dis-tance?), an eight-year-old voice came on the line. "Who do you want?" I replied, "Can you call Edelstein, please?" After another ten minutes I heard Shani's voice. "Did you hear what happened here this week? It was such a shock when this young woman and her child were killed in a traffic accident. But when these things happen, we can't just continue our rou-tine. We have to change something. Roiza, you'd be proud of me. I started a *Shemiras Halashon* campaign. I was so scared. It's not like when you make a speech and people asked you for *Mussar.* I wondered how they would react to my telling them what to do, but it wasn't difficult at all.

"People are hungry. So many *tzaros* are happening out there. People want meaning. You think that because they are fancy ladies they will laugh at you. They end up loving it. You should never hold back on a good thought. Don't say, 'I can't because they will look down on me.' If it is a good deed, the *Ribono shel Olam* will help.

"There was this traffic accident. I got this big circle togeth-er and I said, 'Ladies, you have to listen to this.' I put on Rabbi

Kessin's tape on *Shemiras Halashon*. Now we are learning the *halachos* every day, and when we start talking and I comment that it might be *Lashon Hara*, the people really respond."

The Chofetz Chaim asked me, "Are you a *Kohen*?"

"No," I replied.

He went on, "Maybe you are a *Levi*?"

"No."

"What a pity! *Moshiach* is coming and the *Beis HaMikdash* will be rebuilt. There will be a tremendous yearning to enter the *Beis HaMikdash*. And you are not even a *Levi* who can gain entry into some places. You will be left completely outside. Perhaps you have heard — I'm a *Kohen*. Tell me, why aren't you a *Kohen*?"

I was puzzled by the question. 'Because my father isn't a *Kohen*," I answered.

"And why isn't he a *Kohen*?" he asked further.

The explanation would be the same of course, but I decided not to answer. He obviously had something in mind.

"I'll tell you why," he went on. "Because 3,000 years ago, at the incident of the Golden Calf, your ancestors didn't run when Moshe *Rabbeinu* called out, '*Mi L'Hashem Eilai*, Whoever is with G-d come to me!' My father and all the other *Leviim* ran to Moshe. Your father did not. Now take it to heart. When you hear the call, *Mi L'Hashem Eilai*, come running!"

This is the message of the Chofetz Chaim. We are living in a time when any thinking person can hear a Great *Shofar* blasting from all sides, calling out: *Mi L'Hashem Eilai!* — and it is incumbent on us to come running (Rabbi Shimon Schwab *Z"L, The Jewish Observer,* January 1984).

One definition of courage is a willingness to stand up for our ideals and to risk being different. Any change we contemplate will probably involve sacrificing security. The choice is up to us. If we can allow ourselves to enthusiastically explore new paths, we will be rewarded with more than just a clear conscience. We will have many of our acquaintances joining us and walking alongside in lasting and meaningful friendship.

✍ Interview

Roiza: Some people think it's nothing to call another person "Goody-Goody." How do you feel about it?

Elka: It's not much of a picnic. "Goody-Goody" is one of the worst names people could ever call me. I have often had the urge to do what's right, but I was afraid of being called "Goody-Goody."

Roiza: When did you disagree with the class' actions?

Elka: In fourth grade, most of the girls didn't like the teacher. I thought she was an excellent teacher. The class did a popular trick. They would stand near the window and pretend they didn't know that she had walked in. A few girls, including me, refused to join. It's definitely not a nice thing to do, not to mention it's pure *chutzpah*.

Roiza: Was there a specific time when refusing to join in the class' shenanigans was especially hard?

Elka: I used to dread substitutes because I was afraid of how the class would act. Why! I don't know how to tell you what we did! We made one substitute quit. We called her a horrible name to her face! I wouldn't join the class! I couldn't join them. Most of the time I just couldn't protest, though you don't know how much I wanted to! I cried a lot then. I was very confused and upset. Most of the time I was called "Goody-Goody Elka," even though I didn't protest.

Roiza: Some girls say, "Students have always made trouble for substitutes. What's wrong with a little fun?" What would you answer those girls?

Elka: I also love to have fun, but not if it would make someone miserable! Every day, I pictured myself up there, after I had worked hard preparing the lessons standing in front of a class that's making trouble, and watching the lesson get ruined. Would you like to be treated like a creature from Jupiter?

Roiza: How do you think things would be different if people didn't worry about peer pressure?

Elka: Although a few girls always refuse to join in the trouble, there are probably many more who go along with the shenanigans of the class because they are afraid to be different. If we all were not afraid to speak up, I think those tricks would stop. Maybe some day I won't be afraid. *Elka B.*

Exercise

Imagine a day in your life when you were surrounded by friendliness and peer pressure had disappeared. What would it be like?

_____

_____

Actual Responses

If we didn't worry about peer pressure, we could do what our heart really wants to do. When recess time came and someone began speaking *Lashon Hara,* I could tell her, "No *Lashon Hara,*" and instead of laughing at me, she would spread the word. Soon in the whole school the words "No *Lashon Hara*" would be said. When I'd come home from school, my friends who go to different schools would tell me that they had the same day I had. I wish a day like this would come.

Bracha Leah D.

On the day when friendship reigned, I would talk and be friends with everyone in my class. I would be friends with girls who have good *midos* and things I can learn from. I wouldn't be scared of what my other friends might say. *Ettie P.*

I got to school one day and everything was different. There were no fights. At recess when the jumprope game began, everyone was playing and everyone got a turn. *Miriam A.*

One day everyone stopped speaking *Lashon Hara* and everyone was really friendly. Then *Moshiach* came and everyone was all together. People didn't speak *Lashon Hara.* Instead everyone was happy, talking nicely and being friendly. However, in the morning, everyone spoke *Lashon Hara* and was unfriendly. No one was nice to one another and no one enjoyed it at all. That's when I realized I had just been imagining. *Leah Malka G.*

I woke up and was so happy that it was a nice day. When I looked in my closet, I realized that all my nice new dresses were in the washing machine. It was getting late so I had to start getting dressed quickly. I had to wear an old, yucky gray dress. When I came downstairs, there was no good snack and my mother packed me crackers with peanut butter. How weird! No one eats that anymore. For lunch my mother packed me an avocado sandwich. No one eats that food anymore! I was embarrassed by my "old-fashioned" dress when I came into class. But the girls said, "What a nice outfit you are wearing today, Ruchoma." I was thrilled. At recess and lunch when I took out my food, everyone asked me for a taste. I felt so good. That was the happiest day of my life. *Ruchoma L.*

Nobody wears sneakers to school. Why do I have to? Everybody is going to the mall. Why can't I? Why can't I get an outfit, not only dresses which no one wears? Everyone gets five pairs of shoes a year. Why not me? I'm the only one in the class that has laced-up shoes. Why can't I have slip-ons? I'm the only kid in the class that has to wash the dishes. Why can't I have a break tonight? All the girls in my class go to bed at 10:30, why do I have to be different and go at 10:00? Everyone in my class has a few fancy pencils and I don't have any. Why can't I? Nobody has red uniform blouses like I do. Everyone only wears gingham blouses, why can't I? Do you recognize these statements? They seem to go on in everyone's houses. All these statements are caused by peer pressure. My parents try to convince me that I only need to be embarrassed if I do something wrong or dangerous. If I have an old-fashioned briefcase, that's nothing to be embarrassed of. They suggest I become a P.P.P. — proper, proud person — proud of doing the right things and following what Hashem wants even if it's not what everyone is doing.

This is how I imagine my conversations would go if I didn't worry about peer pressure:

"Ding- a- ling!" rang the phone.

"Yes," I answered.

"Hi! It's me, Sorah. I called to ask you if you could come with me after school to "Toys R Us" half walking and half by train? I am also going with Dena."

"One second. I'll ask my mother."

"Mommy, can I go with the two most popular girls..."

"No, I don't think it's safe, even though their mothers permit it."

"O.K." I said

I picked up the phone again.

"Hello?"

"Hi! Can you go?"

"My mother doesn't think it's safe so I can't."

"O.K., bye!"

If I didn't worry about peer pressure, I wouldn't argue with my mother if she felt that something I wanted to do wasn't safe. On the other hand, if I told my friend "No," she'd accept me as I am and still like me anyway.   *Shoshana F.*

An Imaginary Day With Achdus and Chesed
Miriam B.

One day I came to school
and everyone was so, so nice.
What a surprise!
Everyone was lending a hand,
It was beautiful to see.

After school we went to the nursing home.
We talked and fed the patients.
They loved it so, so, much.
After we made everyone happy we went home.

I thought about today.
I realized that it felt so, so good
To think about giving instead of getting.
I hope it continues like this every day.
If it will —
Perhaps Moshiach will come.

2-Minute Tips
Peer Pressure

1. **You are wonderful just the way you are**
   Are you afraid that you aren't good enough? Instead of putting yourself under pressure, let your unique strengths unfold. Feel the freedom of being yourself.

2. **Rules**
   Don't accept "rules" that you don't feel are right. Ask yourself, "If I follow the crowd, will I feel proud of myself afterwards or will I feel guilty?"

3. **Look for the good**
   Others don't need to be wrong for you or your group to be right. Everyone is doing the best they can right now, including you.

4. **Dress for success**
   Peer pressure might generate a false need for fancy clothes. You will feel better about yourself if your blouse is ironed and if your skirt is clean and pressed. A neat appearance shows that you respect yourself.

5. **Be strong**
   What ideals are important to you? Do you feel that you will defend for your values? Remember your values are your foundations as you grow and mature.

Now I Know!

- Mature people are independent. They can stand by their principles, and they don't need everyone's approval.

- My values make me unique. It may be hard to incorporate ideals into my lifestyle but it's worth it. It will help me become a better person.

- Before I speak up I may worry about peer pressure but afterwards I will see that it worked out OK.

- We are Hashem's children. Hashem notices and has pleasure when we do what is right.

Chapter 13

> מָתַי יַגִּיעוּ מַעֲשַׂי לְמַעֲשֵׂי אֲבוֹתַי . . .
> שֶׁלֹּא קָנוּ הָעוֹלָם הַזֶּה וְהָעוֹלָם הַבָּא אֶלָּא
> בִּשְׁבִיל מַעֲשִׂיהֶם הַטּוֹבִים.

When will my deeds reach the deeds of my ancestors?
They acquired Olam Hazeh and Olam Haba only because of their good deeds.

(Tanna d'Vei Eliyahu Rabbah 23:1)

Spiritual Treasures

here is one aspect of cleaning for Pesach that I look forward to. It's the golden moment when I discover a treasure in the back of a drawer. Suddenly tender memories wash over me. We need to expand our spirit. We need to relieve that claustrophobic feeling that creeps in, by raising our eyes toward the horizon. It can help us get through the day. There is a feeling of lightness and freedom that our gentle memories can give us. We feel hopeful. Beforehand, we were overwhelmed with the dark struggle of barely coping and wondering if there is a good reason to work so hard. Now that little item that we are caressing calms the storm for us.

I discovered the wonderful feeling of release that savoring spiritual treasures can give us when I first began working on this book. Ever since, I began to strive to broaden my spirit and move gently ahead by learning a lesson from any childhood object I have. It's a special way for me to personally connect with goals that have become buried over the years. Once I stretch and warm up my spiritual limbs, I say the prayer of our Sages, "מָתַי יַגִּיעוּ מַעֲשַׂי לְמַעֲשֵׂי אֲבוֹתַי, When will I bring those great deeds to life in the here and now?" It feels wonderful. I am in a private place where inspiration might just become a reality.

If I find something that belonged to my grandmother, I might mimic her noble way of dealing with life for a while. Perhaps for an hour I will be gentle and not raise my voice. After all, Bubby gave a stern look only on occasion and that self-control must be somewhere in my genes. The impression does last for a while. My ancestors are almost here in the room with me.

Rena said, "I grew up in my grandparents' home. My grandmother had certain aphorisms that she always said. When my father was critically ill I repeated the sayings I remembered to him. He always smiled through his pain when he heard it."

Henya said, "I also grew up with my grandmother. We were very close. I asked her once. 'When you are gone, how will I go on with my life?' She answered, 'You will go on because you will remember what I said and through that I will have continuity!' "

This stretching exercise helps me make a conscious decision to go beyond my limitations. I have concentrated on something that distracted me from my problems. Enjoying these spiritual treasures helps me stand tall. I feel ready to confront any hurdle.

Yoshiyahu was the fifth-to-last king before the destruction of the First *Beis HaMikdash*. He began to rectify the evils his predecessors had propagated in the land. In his 18th year, he ordered extensive repairs to the *Beis HaMikdash* under the direction of Chilkiah the High Priest and Shafan the scribe. While he was inspecting the *Beis HaMikdash,* Chilkiah the High Priest discovered a Torah scroll hidden between two rows of stones.

Which Torah scroll was this and why was it hidden? This Torah scroll was written by Moshe *Rabbeinu* himself in the desert. It was about 800 years old. No one had seen it because it had been hidden during Menashe's reign to prevent him from defacing it as he had done to many other Torah scrolls.

When Shafan the scribe saw the Torah scroll, he immediately rushed with it to King Yoshiyahu. The Temple Torah scroll was rolled up before it was stored. One always opened it to the first words of the Torah. This scroll was found rolled to the section dealing with the afflictions in *Devarim*. It said (*Devarim* 28:36), יוֹלֵךְ ה' אֹתְךָ וְאֶת מַלְכְּךָ אֲשֶׁר תָּקִים עָלֶיךָ אֶל גּוֹי אֲשֶׁר לֹא יָדַעְתָּ, *Hashem will lead you and your king whom you will set up over yourself to a nation you never knew* (*Devarim* 28:36). G-d would sentence the Jews to exile for rebelling against Him.

Shafan told the king, "Chilkiah the High Priest gave me this Torah scroll written by Moshe." As Shafan read the words of the afflictions in the Torah, King Yoshiyahu rent his garments.

King Yoshiyahu cared about following in the footsteps of King David. He started to correct the evil of the previous wicked kings. This Torah scroll had a strong impact because it was found in the *Beis HaMikdash* and written by Moshe *Rabbeinu*. The message had a frightening urgency.

This can be compared to someone who suspects he has a serious illness and checks it out. An x-ray that confirms the seriousness of his situation would give him a jolt.

Yoshiyahu said to the High Priest, "Go to Chuldah the prophetess, and inquire of Hashem concerning the words of the Torah which has been found. Hashem's wrath is great, since our forefathers did not obey the words of this scroll to do according to all that is written in it" (*II Melachim* 22:13).

The Sages ask, "Why was Chuldah chosen and not Yirmiyahu?" The king sent them to a woman prophetess because a woman would have mercy and pray to save them from this terrible tragedy.

Chuldah told them that Hashem would bring calamity to this place and upon its inhabitants because they worshiped idols and scorned the pure service of Hashem. Yoshiyahu would be spared. The decree would not happen in his time. "Since your heart has become soft, and you have humbled yourself before Hashem, when you heard what I spoke about this place and about its inhabitants, and you rent your garments and wept before Me, I have heard your cry, said Hashem" (ibid. 22:19).

The *Navi* tells us, "Before him there was no king like him who did *Teshuvah* (returned to Hashem) with all his heart and all his soul and all his possessions. . . and after him none arose like him" (ibid. 23:25). Yoshiyahu destroyed idols, houses of idol worship and pagan altars throughout the land. He abolished the pagan priests and destroyed the houses where enclosures were woven for the *Asheirah*. He made impure the area where Molech sacrifices were done. He broke down monuments to idols. He even destroyed the golden calf that Yerovam ben Nevat had made in Beis-el.

The voice of Hashem called to them from the Torah scroll written by Moshe and they answered. This Torah scroll linked them to the previous generations. They felt they were there in the desert accepting the Torah at Har Sinai.

Gregg's grandfather was the last Rav of Dubno. His father was a Holocaust survivor who turned away from Judaism. Gregg came to Israel and saw a friend from Ohr Somayach; but the meeting was stormy. Gregg thought his friend had gone crazy. Back on the Kibbutz, he broke his ankle and had nothing to do but think. He realized it was time to go back and try it out. A week later someone at the Yeshiva showed him a copy of one of the few remaining sefarim of his grandfather. "This sefer has your name in it on the front page," he said. (Gregg [Gershon] was named after his grandfather.) The introduction ended with a prayer that Torah not depart from his descendants, "And may that be my reward in this world and the next."

(*Jerusalem Echoes*, page 52)

Exercise
The Gems You have

Can you remember the first *siddur* you owned?

_____

_____

What happened when you opened a *Machzor* from the first set of *Machzorim* that had your name in gold on the cover?

_____

_____

Tell a story about a special object.

_____

_____

How did you receive it? Was it a present?

_____

_____

Do you own something that was used by an ancestor?

_____

_____

Responses

I happily danced around my classroom in an ironed white blouse and a blue pleated skirt. My shoes were shiny black and my tights lacy white. All the Pre-1A children around me looked like me. We were all going to get our first *siddur.* In the *siddur* play we sang how happy we are to get our *siddur* and be able to read *Modeh Ani* and *Shema* in a real *siddur*. The principal brought in a pile of *siddurim*. After many girls, my name was called. I kissed my *siddur* affectionately and thanked the principal. I noticed my name stamped in gold lettering on the brown *siddur*. This was truly my own *siddur*. From that day on I always used my *siddur*. Today, although the *siddur* has some scotch-taped papers, I still use it. It will forever be a treasure to me.   *Rochel Esty L.*

The *siddur* on the highest shelf in my grandparents' bookcase seemed to have witnessed an old, silent story. Very carefully I picked it up and slowly opened the front cover. My grandfather's name and birthplace were written in European handwriting inside. My grandfather walked into the room, and saw me holding his *siddur*. "You know, that was my *siddur* back in the old country," he said.

"Wow," I said, "can I use it?"

"Of course. What else is a *siddur* for if not to pray from it?"

That morning I *davened Shacharis* with more concentration than ever before. The *siddur* held secrets of years long gone. It's a priceless treasure.   *Rechy F.*

On Rosh Hashanah when I was *Bas Mitzvah*, I got a leather-bound *siddur* for my present. It has gold edging around the pages and gold corners. When I use this beautiful *siddur*, my *tefillos* are said with more concentration.   *Chaya Sara R.*

Recently a gem turned up in our family. This gem is not a jewel or a piece of old silver, but rather a simple volume of *Mishnayos* that belonged to my great-grandfather. When my grandfather survived the Holocaust, he found nothing was left of his home after the war. Everything was destroyed or taken away.

Last year a friend of my grandfather visited Chust, Czechoslovakia, my grandfather's home town. While poking around in the *shul,* he came upon a pile of old *sefarim.* He noticed my grandfather's name written on the flyleaf of one *sefer* and brought it back with him to my grandfather. Finally, we have a tangible link to the past.   *Tziporah B.*

The doorbell rang and my six-year-old sister ran into our house, proudly holding a brand-new velvet *siddur.* When I watched my sister's exuberance, I found myself remembering my own first *siddur.* I remember how thankfully I *davened* out of my first *siddur,* and then carefully placed it in our wooden *sefarim* "shrank." Today my *siddur* is old and worn from so much use, yet I love it even more now.   *Esty F.*

Each Shabbos when we stand up for *Kiddush* my father places my great-grandfather's *becher* in his hand. A surge of family pride wells up inside me as I think of all my great-grandfather went through to keep this *Kiddush* cup and Shabbos holy.   *Sarala Z.*

We inherited a *siddur* that my grandfather *Z"TL* used all his life. He used it constantly. Very often, he would say *Tehillim* from the *siddur.* The *siddur* is a little crumpled and looks very old. The tears can be seen on the *siddur's* pages. When we use this *siddur,* we feel the emotions that it absorbed and we can almost hear his voice. We *daven* with more feeling when we use this *siddur.*

What about us ? We hope that our feelings when we *daven* will also be absorbed by this heirloom *siddur.* We hope that our descendants will also get our positive emotions out of the *siddur* just like we got our grandfather's *Z"TL.*   *Yehudis S.*

I hugged the *Tehillim* tightly to me, I ran my hand over its leather-bound cover. I thought of the many ancestors who had used it before me. Did they feel safe and happy while holding it? It was a gift from my grandmother. She told me to cherish it and safeguard it for future generations to come. "Do not be mistaken," she told me, "it is not the cover that makes it special, but the words you will say and the feeling of gratitude you will feel to your Creator." As the words of prayer dance before my eyes, I promise myself to be worthy of a most precious gift.   *Sara H.*

This past Pesach my grandmother came from Israel and gave me a beautiful white-leather *siddur* with my name on it. A *siddur* with your name on it is important to a person. When you *daven* from it, you have a special feeling. You try to handle it with better care and even if you want to give it away, you can't.

I remembered a story that someone told me about an older woman who always *davened* from the same *siddur*. All her tears of joy and sadness were in it. I started thinking of me in my old age with my *siddur*.   *Meital R.*

During World War II my grandfather and great-uncle ran away from their home in Cracow, Poland. They were in many different places during the war, including a labor camp in Siberia. Through it all my grandfather held on to his precious *Tefillin* and put them on every day. These *Tefillin* are still with us today.   *Chavie W.*

How many people *bentsch* on your *esrog* and *lulav*? You and your children? Literally hundreds of people used ours. No, they didn't come to our home. My older brother would rush out after the *seudah* on *Yom Tov* and during

Chol HaMoed to stop people in the street.

I can remember standing in the street, a shy impatient young boy, as my older brother would stop, question, and then instruct a passerby. Even on the way home from *shul,* he would be catching these *mitzvos.* But what impressed me more than my brother's bravery was the occasional tear I would notice in the corner of an older man's eye as he looked nostalgically at the odd yet familiar sight of a *lulav* and *esrog.*

(The Jewish Observer)

An 11-year-old girl tells me this story: "This summer in camp I always shared the snacks I bought at the canteen, but if you wanted a potato chip you had to say the *berachah* out loud, so that I and anyone else nearby could answer *Amein."*

My cousin's elderly neighbor gave her beautiful antique candlesticks. They were in the neighbor's family for many generations. She told my cousin, "I have no one to give them to." Now my cousin uses them every Shabbos. The neighbor wasn't religious. I think that the candlesticks are smiling. If the candlesticks could speak, they would say that they are happy to be used for a *mitzvah* again.

2-Minute Tips
Spiritual Treasures

1. **Be Alert**
   How many Shabbos meals has your oldest *Kiddush* cup seen? What struggles and joys did your *siddur* witness? Just thinking about these things helps make *mitzvos* more meaningful.

2. **Start a Scrapbook/Album**
   Almost by accident about 14 years ago, I began saving my letters in an album. Many of the letters in it are irreplaceable. Some letters remind me about precious milestones in my life.

3. **Collect Stories**
   Hashgachah Pratis, Gam Zu L'Tovah, weddings, family celebrations, even the story of when you were born; stories can help us feel closer to our relatives and add meaning to our "spiritual treasures."

4. **Use It!**
   Don't just leave the precious item in the back of your closet. Use it and think about it.

   My mother gave me Bubby's bronze candlesticks. They are old and ornate with square bases. My mother said, "I will only give them to you on the condition that you keep them polished."

Now I Know!

● Spiritual treasures are more meaningful if I think about them and use them.

● Spiritual treasures are a tangible reminder for important ideals — like my priorities, goals, and values.

● Right now I can think of something I would like to remember a number of times a day. Which treasure will I choose that can serve as a reminder?

Chapter 14

" **Mom Wanted!**

Long hours, low pay, little time off.
Must be willing to work overtime
on weekends, holidays, and summer vaca-
tion. Energy, imagination,
intelligence, endurance, and flexibility
required. Must have ability to lead, instruct
and guide, coupled with a
warm, loving, affectionate personality.
On-the-job training offered. "

Family Relationships

✍ Inventory

1. I spend most of my time at night on homework and tests.
2. School pressures make me nervous around my family.
3. I cannot really listen to my mother when I'm worried about someone who insulted me.
4. I'd like to help more for Shabbos but I usually am too busy catching up at the end of the week.
5. I spend my days off almost exclusively with friends.
6. I ask my friends for advice on crucial issues.
7. I can't communicate deep feelings without yelling.
8. I rarely compliment my parents.

9. I feel nervous on Shabbos. I don't know why.

10. I feel uncomfortable talking about my family's unique values.

*I*f you checked more than two of the above questions, you should re-evaluate your priorities. It often takes thought to find the balance when you are growing up. Craving for independence and social success can sometimes overshadow your respect for who you already are.

Ruthie is 11 years old. She is the shortest in her class. She does well on tests but often gets into trouble for forgetting her homework and misplacing everything from gloves to library cards. Ruthie wants the grownups in her life to stop nagging and to trust her.

Grownups don't understand. Her mother sees her settling down on Shabbos with a good book and says, "Why don't you go to your friend's house?" But Ruthie hasn't found a friend who respects her just the way she is. Ruthie wants to be popular. The popular girls ignore her. She doesn't have the "in" clothes or the "in" pencil case and briefcase. Her mother thinks that those things are a waste of money. Ruthie thinks that if she had a fashionable briefcase and stylish clothes the popular girls would notice her. When something spills or when she leaves her clothes and books lying around, her mother usually gets very angry. Ruthie gets upset too, "My mother blames everything on me. I didn't do it on purpose. Why is my mother making such a big deal about every little mess?"

Ruthie wonders, "I know my mother loves me, but why doesn't she tell me when she's proud of me? Why does she criticize me so much and give so many orders?"

✒ Comments

In this space, describe a time that something similar happened to you.

_____

_____

_____

_____

You have now reached a stage where you know that growth is possible. You may be planning how you will overcome some of the burdensome problems that you face every day with the new ideas you've learned. Now we will discuss how we can apply these ideas in the home zone.

✒ Do you want to know —

● How can we really feel close to our parents when we are doing things together?
● What should we work on to avoid hurting our parents' feelings?
● What are the most powerful moments of the day?
● How can we avoid conflict with our parents?
● Why is it important to say, "Thank you"?

The _mitzvah_ of listening to parents becomes complicated for teenagers. We want to obey, but we also want to have our way. In this chapter we will discuss improving family relationships.

✒ Developing Real Closeness

A caring person is able to listen to others with respect, sensitivity, concentration, and thoughtfulness — you have the potential to be this caring person. On a scale of one to ten, how caring are you?

Do you listen when adults talk to you or do you only pretend to listen? Do you show respect by coming when someone calls you or do they have to wait for you? When you are walking with your mother, do you listen courteously or are you busy daydreaming?

We all have the ability to connect with our parents. It requires respect, a willingness to listen 100 percent, and the urge to share a part of ourselves — three qualities that are available to us all.

Often, our closeness to our parents is demonstrated quite humbly. It is pretty much unannounced, without fanfare, yet in small ways it makes family life a little more pleasant. Remember little triumphs and details to share. Celebrate each new discovery in school and each *Rashi* you read well. Serve your mother a coffee and sit down and have your snack together. Go for a walk together and listen attentively. Buy your mother's favorite treat in the bakery on your way home from school. Say something cheerful while you help with the dishes. These are just a few of the ways we can give our parents *Nachas*.

You have probably done all these things already, but if they are to be a priority you have to become aware of the importance of respecting parents in this way. In order to make each day worthwhile, we must know what we are doing, and why. The *Yalkut Meam Loez* stresses the great merit of honoring parents on a daily basis.

"Yaakov *Avinu* had many sons but when they got older, each one left home to live in his own place. Binyamin, the youngest son, stayed with his father. Binyamin ate with his father and drank with him. When they went out, Yaakov and Binyamin walked together and Yaakov *Avinu* would lean on Binyamin's shoulder. Hashem said, "In the place that the *tzaddik* Yaakov rested his arm I will dwell" — as it says (*Devarim* 33:12) וּבֵין כְּתֵפָיו שָׁכֵן, *and rests between his shoulders*. The

Beis HaMikdash (Temple) was on Mount Moriah on the "shoulders" of Binyamin's portion in *Eretz Yisrael*.

Recognize that your caring gestures are truly important. As you explore new ways to show your parents your love and respect, you will feel a greater closeness with them. Start by spending some really connected time with your parents for at least five minutes twice a day.

✌ Avoiding Hurt Feelings

Suri admitted, "Most of my friends like their parents a lot, but we all complain about them anyway. Everyone does it."

Suri knows it's *Lashon Hara* when she gets on the phone and complains about her parents' unfair rules. Why does she do it? When Suri is upset, she feels an irresistible longing to talk. Her friend will understand and, after all, Suri is feeling so miserable. She doesn't intend to hurt her parents but her pain blocks her view of how harmful it is. Perhaps her parents can't hear the words she is saying into the phone but they can guess what she is saying.

When we are feeling hurt or angry, we can't think clearly. We feel that if we are upset, then it's excusable if we hurt others. Perhaps if we realize how important it is to take precautions not to hurt our parents, we will change this thought pattern.

> At the Akeidah, Yitzchak said, "Father, bind me lest I kick with my feet and strike you." At the most awesome moment of his life, when he was about to give up his life to Hashem, Yitzchak's thoughts focused on how to avert the accidental dishonoring of his father.
>
> (*Rav Moshe Speaks*, Rav Moshe Sternbuch)

We all refer to *Akeidas Yitzchak* as a special merit at the beginning of the year when we ask Hashem for a good year on Rosh Hashanah. What does *Akeidah* mean? What happened at the *Akeidah*? *Akeidah* means to tie. Yitzchak was never sacrificed, he was only tied on to the altar. This precaution of

Yitzchak not to hurt his father, even unintentionally, shows us Yitzchak's greatness of character. And it is our merit for thousands of years.

Our parents are always there for us — to comfort, reassure, and show us unconditional love. They always encourage us to try again. Sometimes at the same time that we protest their "No," we are secretly relieved that some of the pressure is taken off. Let's not complain about them to our friends.

The Most Powerful Moments of the Day

A person should always rush to greet his father and mother, his teachers who taught him Torah and Mishnah, and every person in the world. As we say of Rabban Yochanan Ben Zakkai, no person ever greeted him first, not even a gentile in the marketplace (*Tanna d'Vei Eliyahu*).

What are the most powerful moments of the day? They are the last five minutes before you part in the morning and the first five minutes when your parent comes home at night. All day your parents will remember that smile at the door in the morning and they will look forward to seeing your cheerful face when they come home at night. Say Hello (and Goodbye) first! Start off your day with a smile and a blessing for your parents to have a nice day, and give your parents a cheerful welcome every evening.

The *Yalkut Meam Loez* says:

> *Rav Avahu said that his son performs the mitzvah of kibud av. Rav Avimi, his son, had five grown sons during the lifetime of his father Rav Avahu. Yet when Rav Avahu, his father, came and knocked on the door, Rav Avimi would run and open the door himself and he wouldn't allow any of his sons to open the door for his father. He would call, "My master, I'm coming right away; my master, I'm coming right away."*

✌ Avoiding Conflict

At 7:14 in the morning I heard a loud crash, glass splinter-ing, and the screech of brakes. Two cars had collided on my corner. Both drivers were unharmed; in fact, they both jumped out of their cars and began a high-pitched argument. "It was my right of way — you should have stopped," said one driver.

"I did stop to look, but I didn't see you coming. You were speeding," countered the second driver.

An accident is destructive on several fronts and it could have been avoided. First of all, each driver assumed that the other person would yield the right of way to him. Have you ever paused at a stop sign for a second and thought to your-self, "That car is a little close but he'll slow down when he sees me"? Second, even if one driver did have the right of way, stopping for a few seconds would have saved him from a lot of distress.

When we stop to consider the other person's point of view and concede to him, we have done something of great value. *Rashi* explains (*Shemos* 15:12) that Pharaoh merited a prop-er burial, because in one instance, he admitted that Hashem was right. Although this positive act had long since been over-shadowed by the impact of Pharaoh's wicked actions, it was not forgotten. Hashem recorded it in the Torah, acknowledged it, and rewarded Pharaoh.

Am I honestly *always* totally right? Did I provoke the argu-ment by my actions, tone of voice, or facial expressions?

Family relationships are hardest to work on because with family we are most vulnerable. Family members see each other every day, in all types of situations. Another struggle that family members deal with is the issue of conflicts that repeat themselves over and over again.

How can we deal with different opinions? The first step is to talk together. Remember however that talking TOGETHER means that both parties *listen* at least as much as they talk. The second step is to remember that family members are allies, who support one another. The third step is to earnestly attempt to find a compromise.

When we listen and open our hearts to understand another person and accept their unique personality, then compromise is possible.

Rabbi Yissachar Frand explains that the *Mezuzah* teaches us that compromise is the foundation of the Jewish home. "Why is the *Mezuzah* positioned on the doorway at an angle? There is a difference of opinion in the Talmud. One point of view is that the *Mezuzah* should be vertical. The other point of view is that the Mezuzah should be horizontal. The *Halachah* in this case arrives at a compromise and we put the *Mezuzah* on a slant — diagonally. I think that the Mezuzah is sending us a message. The *Mezuzah* is the first thing that you see when you walk into your home. It conveys the critical information, 'Don't be rigid, you can't always have your way. You have to bend and make adjustments. After all, that is what *Shalom* is all about.' "

Do you sometimes sulk behind closed doors because someone should be listening to you, but they aren't? When we are right, but it's necessary to overcome a communication problem, it's helpful to consider other points of view. Ask yourself how you would want someone to deal with you after you've erred. As our Sages said, "Whoever judges another person favorably, will be judged with sympathy" (*Shabbos* 127b). In fact, every now and then we can successfully solve a problem with sympathy and empathy alone. In the following interview, Ita, a participant in one of my workshops, describes how she solved a common problem.

✍ Interview

Roiza: The people who are most important to us may disagree with us at times. Has this ever happened to you?

Ita: I can work really hard to clean the shag carpet in my living room and in just half an hour my four-year-old brother can have it covered with zillions of teensy pieces of paper and hundreds of tiny Lego blocks. I say to him, "If you are big enough to make the mess, you are big enough to clean it up." However, when I return after five minutes, he only picked up two blocks and three pieces of paper and is just sitting on the side and daydreaming. When he notices me he pleads, "Ita, I can't do it by myself." I usually end up helping, but I scold him too, "You made the mess without any help, didn't you?"

Roiza: Your brother feels he needs your help, but you feel he can clean up on his own. What happened to help you see his point of view?

Ita: One afternoon when I was picking up these toys, I remembered that two years ago I made a surprise party for a friend. Many people came. The next day I woke up to an overwhelming mess in the house. Of course the room where the party took place was messy, but because my sisters and brothers played everywhere and carried food around, every corner in every room was cluttered.

I told my mother, " I need help cleaning all this up." It was just an overwhelming mess.

Roiza: How did this recollection help you understand your brother better?

Ita: I put myself in my brother's shoes and realized how he must feel when he sees little papers all over the place and he just can't cope with the job of picking it up. I also remembered that although I was responsible for the mess when I made the party, it had been too much for me to handle alone as well.

Roiza: What did you decide to do as a result of this?

Ita: I decided to help without scolding as long as I see that he is also working with me. I also decided to show him how to play and be a little neater. For example, when I see he wants to cut papers into tiny bits, I bring a little pail and tell him to cut over the pail.

Roiza: What makes you want to act thoughtfully ?

Ita: I feel that it is easier to speak to children and to anyone when you try to see the other person's point of view. I also believe that it's important to be compassionate. Have you ever gone to a doctor's office? You sit there waiting alone in the examining room. The nurse says, "The doctor will be with you in a minute." In reality he comes in after 20 minutes have passed. Think about that the next time a kid wants a drink and you say, "In a minute."

✐ Thank You!

Of course mothers and daughters really do care about each other and love each other. Somehow we never get around to saying it. We make the mistake of thinking that it doesn't need to be said because it is something that every-one knows already. However if we forget to say thank you but do complain loudly, what ends up happening is that both mothers and daughters start to feel awful. It's important for children to thank parents and for parents to thank children every day. This is also true of saying something nice or encouraging.

Even the most confident person feels shy about telling their deep feelings to someone. If you don't write a letter once in a while, those beautiful grateful feelings will just dry up and blow away.

A letter is such a precious gift. You notice it laying under the door with the handwritten address on it, in an envelope that isn't a bill. It waits for you after you trudged home from a long day of toil and trouble. Your words don't need to be poetry, they just need to be sincere. Your mother can read it twice and again tomorrow, "Mommy, you are such a great mother to have, to love and especially to be with."

When we write, people can know who we really are and what we sincerely think. Otherwise, people will just remember us as a good girl. On the page we can express what is deep in our hearts, and thereby feel much closer. These feelings are often difficult to verbalize, so writing helps.

The first step to writing a letter is to be prepared with the necessary supplies — stationery, pens, and markers for adding a sketch or two.

A letter is a gift that you may feel like giving any day, so it pays to be ready. In your letter tell your mother what you are doing and write as though you were talking to her. Don't worry about grammar — it's truly not important here. Where did you go today, what did they say, what did you think about it? What reminded you of home?

If you don't know how to begin, start with where you are right now. "I'm sitting on the top bunkbed looking out the window. Everyone ran outside to play punchball. I was thinking how nice it is that you wait for me so often by the window when I come home."

Probably your mother will put your letters away. She'll read them again and again, and next year they will sound even better than they do now. One day she might show them to your children. "This is the letter your mommy wrote when she was just as old as you." Your letter will be an antique. It will remind your children who have helicopters in their driveways that once people drove ordinary cars! Your simple description of what you did, where you stayed, and who you saw will give the children of the future a picture of how you feel right now.

So pick up a piece of paper and write that letter!

Exercise

Thank your parent for a specific incident that you really enjoyed.

Dear Mother,

_____

_____

_____

Actual Responses
Letters Girls Wrote to Their Mothers

Thank you, Mommy, for teaching me the right way to act. If I'm doing something wrong, you correct me. I don't always change and do the right thing the first time you tell me, but after awhile I do the right thing. You taught me prayers and *Shema*. I knew the *Shema* since I was around three years old. Also Mommy, I never saw you get angry about petty things. You only get angry and upset about important things, like when your children are doing the wrong things. Mommy, you are such a great mother to have, to love, and especially to be with. Sometimes you even take me places, only you and I. Thank you for being my mother.   *Ruchoma L.*

Today, I thank you for being my mother. Ema, I love your ideas that you sometimes give me for a project. They are fantastic and they get me good marks. You also give us good ideas for our doll house. You make different things for the doll house. When I'm bored, you think of brilliant things to do. When I was eight, we made yarn dolls for my birthday party. Everybody went home with a nice little yarn doll that my very own mother thought of. Even though we made the yarn dolls when I was eight, and now I'm eleven, I still think it was great. I also love your drawings. You made me a really nice picture with my name on it. Besides, if you didn't know how to make nice Hebrew letters, I'd be lost. So I thank you so dearly for everything and I love you.   *Bracha Leah D.*

My mother is so very kind,
When things we lose she always finds.
My mother is a very good cook,
When she's baking, she doesn't peek into the recipe book.

All her food is just great,
Especially her cookies — they are top rate!
My house is very neat, as you can see,
Because my mother scrubs it, until it's shiny!
I really think my mother's the best,
If there will be a contest,
She'll win over the rest!
I'm convinced there is no other
That can take the place of my dear MOTHER! !

Rivka B.

It was in camp that I first appreciated who you really are. In camp there are no home-cooked meals, and laundry is never back when you need it. When I'm sick in camp, there is no one besides the nurse to help me. Whenever I'm sick at home, you help me; you take care of me and you help me make up my schoolwork. Whenever I'm upset, you calm me and help me. When I'm discouraged, you encourage me. You help me with my schoolwork. You are always there when I need you. Thank you is nothing compared to all the things you do for me.

Shulamis W.

There are a countless amount of things I could thank you for — I can't list them all. You buy me everything I could ever need and sometimes you buy me things some could only wish for. You take me to wonderful places on *Chol HaMoed* and other times. Mommy, I can't thank you enough.   *Elky B.*

As I write this thank-you letter, I remember all the good times we have had together. I love to bake. The first time I decided to bake, I asked you, Mommy. You agreed! So out came the mixer and all the ingredients. Now, it's not that easy to bake, so you helped me. Boy, was it fun baking together!

One night I went to sleep very late because we played ana-grams. In and out went my hand as I sat at the table picking out the pieces from the gray worn-out bag. After we finished, I counted and counted until I reached the total. It was a tie! We went to 86th Street to buy my friend a birthday present. Finally, we found just the right thing. It had a pad, pencil, a place for two pictures, and a mirror. As we walked, we talked about all sorts of things. *Rusi H.*

Mommy, I can't believe the way you don't get tired of doing it all for me. I also want to thank you for the things you taught me, like baking cakes, *challos,* and cooking. I feel very close to you, Mommy, and I know that I could tell you anything! *Chasie Z.*

I have never tried being a mother. It sure looks hard. You do a terrific job at it. You work hard a whole day. I don't know if you notice, Mommy, but you never sit down to rest. From the beginning of the day until you go to sleep, you go on doing things for me. When I grow up, I hope to be a wonderful moth-er just like you are. *Rifkie L.*

You are a caring mother, always there, standing by my side ready to lend a hand. You are the one who comforts me when I'm upset. You encourage me if there is a need. You share the pain with me when I'm hurt and congratulate me when I suc-ceed. If I am sick, you are the one who nurses me back to health. You teach me what is right and wrong. You watched me grow and saw my very first movements. We have spent many happy moments together. If not for you, I wouldn't be me. Thank you for just being my mother.

I would like to thank you for letting me go to school. If I wouldn't go to school, then I wouldn't know anything and I wouldn't have so many nice friends. You let me invite friends on Shabbos, so I shouldn't be alone. *Leah Malka G.*

Mommy, If I would sit down to write everything you do, I would never finish. At night I sleep with Eliyahu. He wakes up in the middle of the night. I take him to the bathroom and put him back to sleep. A few minutes after I just fall back asleep, he wakes up for a bottle. I'm so tired. I'm not in the mood of getting out of bed again. Suddenly you are there. You come to the rescue. *Mindel B. R.*

You nurture me tenderly as I grow slowly from childhood into adolescence and onward, *IYH.* You cry with me as I recount my failures; laugh along in my moments of bliss. You make me feel special, so special, that at times I think I am the only child in our family of eight. You taught me the art of giving. I learned to be happy that I wasn't a taker, and to feel joy and accomplishment as the generous one. Thank you for everything. *Laya W.*

I'm writing this letter now, to say the things that I've always left unsaid. Do I show you enough how much I love you? Did I ever thank you, that among a family of 11, I still receive equal care and love? Even in the most hectic moment, you still have the time for a reassuring smile, or a heartfelt thank-you for what I've just done. When ever I do a small favor, I receive in return a thank-you, while you do so much as a mother and do you ever receive that two-worded message that means so much?

Thank you for a home full of *shalom*. You raise your voice only when your must. It plays an integral part in my life. I hope when I am a mother, *IYH,* every one of my children will be treated with equal love and all of the children will be happy.

Shaindy J.

I remember those nights, as you sat beside my bed, and we talked. After our long discussion, you ever so gently raised my right hand above my eyelids, as we recited *Shema Yisrael* together. And then, I felt a light kiss on my cheek as I was falling asleep. In the morning I would awaken and find you, Ema, once again at my bedside with a cup of water and bowl for *netilas yadayim.* It seemed then, Ema, that you waited there the entire night for me to arise. I remember singing *Modeh Ani* with you. You would dress me in my freshly starched clothes, brush my hair, and serve me breakfast. As I stood outside, waiting for my bus, snack in hand, I remember looking up to our window and seeing you, as you watched me go off to school. Ema, you were proud to have a little girl like me, and believe it or not, I was proud to have an Ema like you, too!

You have made me what I am today! Only with the courage you've instilled in me, can I rise and shine, giving you true *nachas.* Only with the *Emunah* and *Ahavas Hashem* which you have established within me can I look ahead to tomorrow. I am indebted to you, Ema, and I promise to carry it all on.

Hindy R.

Do you remember? How could you forget the time I ate a bar of soap or broke your crystal vase, and you carefully checked to see if I had any cuts or bruises before rebuking me? Remember all the times I drew you pictures and you acted as though they were the most valuable things in the world. How could I forget all the times you listened to my imaginary fears and consoled me? You instilled in me confidence and gave me a sense of self. I hope I will bring you much joy and happiness so that one day you may receive the satisfaction you deserve. *Sara H.*

I'm sending you this letter to say the words I can't even express. You said *Shema* with me at night and told me bedtime stories. You crammed with me for midterms and hard tests. When I came off the bus crying and depressed, you calmed me down. When I came home hungry because the school lunch was awful, your delicious supper was waiting at the table. With every passing day there is more to thank you for. Mother, everything you do not only builds your home but it builds my future home too. *Gitty R.*

When I was lost, confused or scared, you were there. When I was frustrated or upset, I could cuddle up in your lap and share my thoughts with you. Sometimes I was thoughtless or disagreed with you. I still felt I love you but I couldn't say it, but you helped me work out my quandaries.

You always have a smile on your face when I come home. Even if you had a rough day, you never speak to me in a rough tone of voice.

No one can every take your place. *Leah S.*

Mommy, you always are there to help me. My first problems were with blocks — when my tower kept falling down, you were the one who rebuilt it again. You helped mealtime pass by reading my favorite books to me. As I got older, my younger brothers and sisters were born, meaning more fights. You showed us how to get along and told us fighting was wrong. Now when I face tests and homework, you stay up at night to study with me.

I've taken many things for granted. I realize now that all these things are very important. *Chaya Rivky S.*

2-Minute Tips
Family Relationships

1. **Ideal You**

   Make a mental picture of the ideal you. Hold that image in mind before you speak and begin acting accordingly.

2. **Listen**

   When you talk to your parents, do your conversations revolve around *you*? Do you find yourself describing only *your* needs, frustrations and disagreements? Start a conversation with your parents about how *their* day went.

3. **Growing Love**

   Love grows when you give it away. How can you lend a helping hand? Remember how happy you feel when you help a friend in need. Offer to help out at home before your parents ask. Make a cup of tea or clear the table with a smile. It will give your mother a tremendous lift.

4. **Do Something Together**

   Think of new things you can do with your family. Perhaps your mother can teach you something that she's good at. Perhaps you can both develop a new hobby together.

Chapter 15

> When my mother grew up in pre-war Poland, she was restless and imagined how wonderful it would be to leave her small town of Dubno, Poland and see the world. She spoke to her mother about all the wonderful places she would visit, the sights she would see, the history she would discover, and the knowledge she would gain.
>
> My grandmother A"H smiled and said, "Yes, my child, it is good to go out on your own. It is good to see, to explore and to grow. It is good to become independent. . . **As long as you have a place to come home to.**"
>
> Did my mother ever imagine how much of the world she would see, how many airplane flights she would take to all the corners of the globe? Did she ever dream that she would one day live in America and benefit from a wonderland of modern conveniences? But she was never able to return to her home, to a Dubno that is no more.

Coming Home

Home is a place where you can share your deepest feelings and you know people care. After trying so hard for so long to be like everyone else, you wake up one day and understand how special it is to be yourself. It feels so comfortable to know others are waiting for you and you don't need an invitation and you don't have to pretend. You walk up the path and everyone runs to the door joyously calling your name. The feeling of closeness gives you strength and makes life's struggle easier.

Your home is at the core of your life. It's a good feeling to wake up in the morning and know who you are and what your goal is for that day. Rebbetzin Esther Greenberg said, "Wake up in the morning and formally invite Hashem's presence into your home. Where there is peace, the *Shechinah* (Hashem's presence) dwells. Today you won't raise your voice or speak gossip. Today you will be patient and Hashem will be with you."

The Torah teaches that when one does God's will, it makes no difference if the act is helping your sister say *Modeh Ani* in the privacy of your home or if it is having the main part in a play performed for *Tzedakah*. Both acts are infinitely valuable. In fact, good deeds done in private have the extra value of being solely for Hashem and not for honor.

Elkanah was a prophet. He was the father of Shmuel the prophet who is described by King David as being equal to Moshe and Aharon. The Sages describe his ascent to leadership. First he advanced in his home. People admired his private life and began following his advice in his neighborhood. After that, his influence rose in the city. Hashem saw his noble spirit and made his name known in all of the land of Israel. Nevertheless, his rise in influence was because of his essential qualities. As the *Zayis Raanan* explains, "It was not because of wealth and not because of lineage, but because of his great deeds."

Elkanah advanced first in his home and you can too. It doesn't matter that no one sees your compassion and generosity. You are becoming a better person and Hashem sees. Privately, be your best. Ask yourself whom you can affect in a positive way today. Those simple actions are the ladder to greatness. Hey, you never know!

⌇ Thank You

I sneaked the present into the room
And set it down carefully on the already crowded table.
As I join my adorably sweet, pint-sized cousin,
her eyes keep glancing at her birthday presents
All wrapped up on the table.
Then she sees it,

Wrapped in shiny paper,
Topped with a big green bow,
it stands out.
A smile creeps upon her lips.
The little pudgy hands rip the glittery paper apart.
She quickly opens the box
next —
A gasp and then a giggle escape her lips
She runs up to me and plants a big wet kiss,
Running off to display her new treasure to her
pint-sized friends.

Rochel B.

Every Succos, Reb Chanoch Henoch of Alexander, a famous Chassidic rebbe, told this story at the last "tisch" (Yom Tov meal) with his Chassidim.

There once was a poor man from Cracow by the name of Reb Aizik Reb Yekeles. Until recent years, the synagogue that he built stood in Cracow, and it was called the shul of Reb Aizik Reb Yekeles. (My father prayed in that shul with the Bobover Rebbe Z"L before World War II.)

One night he dreamt that there was a treasure buried near the royal palace, under the main bridge in Prague. He packed his bags and began the journey to Prague. He was so poor that he couldn't even afford to pay for traveling expenses. He walked and begged for rides on the way. About a month later, he reached Prague.

He was hopeful at first, but soon he noticed that the bridge was guarded for 24 hours a day. How would he ever be able to get to his spot and dig for the treasure?

After a week of waiting, he approached the guard.

"Sir, I had a dream that there is a treasure in this spot under the bridge. If you allow me to dig, we can share the treasure."

The guard laughed, "Do you really believe in dreams? What nonsense! I had a dream that in the

home of a poor Jew, called Reb Aizik Reb Yekeles, a
treasure is buried inside the fireplace. Do you think I
would be so foolish as to pack my bags and make the
journey to Cracow?"

Now Reb Aizik understood why he had to come all
the way to Prague. He turned around and traveled
back home. He began digging under his fireplace. He
found the treasure. With a part of the money, he built
the shul that bore his name.

"And so it is," Reb Chanoch Henoch would say in
the name of Reb Simchah Bunem of Pshis'cha," with
anyone setting out to visit a rebbe. When he returns, his
task is to dig and seek the treasure in his own home
and in his own soul.   (A Treasury of Chassidic Tales,
Rabbi Shlomo Yosef Zevin)

There is something precious that you already have.
However, you only find out that you had it all along, after you
have searched for it all over the world. When we search for
wisdom far away, the riches that are in our home are revealed.
Until now they faded into the background but now they
become important.

Every detail of your home teaches a lesson. Every little
thing you grew up with can influence your life in a big way.
One cannot embroider a tablecloth in an hour, but each little
stitch adds to the whole until the colorful, lively pattern is
complete. When you are forming the design of your life,
incorporate the little rituals you learned as you grew up. They
will fill your life with color and beauty.

Why do I hear the *sefarim* call to me from the shelf, "Are you
using me well?"

I remember. I am about 13 years old. I am standing in the
sefarim store with my father. My father says, "I will buy you
any *sefer* you choose, but you have to learn from it. When you
are learning from it every day for a while, we'll come back and
you can pick another."

Now when I look at the *sefarim* in the bookcase and I

realize that I haven't looked at some of them for quite a while, I hear my father's gentle reminder in my mind, "You have to learn from it every day. . ."

As we mature, we gain an increased ability to see the whole picture. A good question reveals the answer. Necessity causes innovation to bloom. So too, the many little things we didn't notice and never thought about become important to us when we are faced with life's challenges. We learn to appreciate what we already have.

- There are some *mitzvos* you do beautifully. Why do you care so much about those specific *mitzvos*?
- There are times when you feel vulnerable and ask yourself, "What would my parents do now?"
- There are times when you are proud of an accomplishment and someone says, "You remind me of your mother."
- Tears will come to your eyes in *shul* at *Rosh Chodesh Bentching* — because they are singing your father's favorite *nigun*.
- You catch a memory that has lain dormant in the corners of your mind and it changes your outlook on life.

When you struggle for independence and you want to grow up and be *your own person,* don't forget to carry along a piece of home inside you! Be proud of who you are and where you came from.

A Happier You is a little book with big ideas. It is written to inspire you and to direct you to be happier with yourself. This book has also been written to help you think deeply, to look at your beliefs, ideas, feelings, and goals in life.

In this book I have shared with you what I have learned, what I know and what has worked for me and the hundreds of people I've taught. Now it's your turn. I hope that through this book you will feel inspired to find your own path. As you search for the treasures and discoveries all around you, discover the treasures that are inside you as well.

Index

About the Author

Roiza Devorah Weinreich, best selling author of *There Will Never Be Another You,* and *In-Joy,* has designed and presented practical workshops based on Torah principles and true success stories for the past ten years. There are workshops about parenting and dealing with stress for mothers, and on building confidence for teens. If you are interested in more information or if you would like to order the weekly newsletter, send a self-addressed envelope to: Roiza Weinreich, 625 Avenue L, Brooklyn N.Y. 11230.

This volume is part of
THE ARTSCROLLSERIES®
an ongoing project of
translations, commentaries and expositions
on Scripture, Mishnah, Talmud, Halachah,
liturgy, history, the classic Rabbinic writings,
biographies, and thought.

For a brochure of current publications
visit your local Hebrew bookseller
or contact the publisher:

Mesorah Publications, ltd.

4401 Second Avenue
Brooklyn, New York 11232
(718) 921-9000